The Unspeakable Free Gift

The Unspeakable Free Gift

The Power of God's Spirit Indwelling the Christian

By Keith Petersen

This book is dedicated to the myriad of men and women—Old Testament and New Testament saints—who have faithfully served God, and to Dad and Mom—two Christians who delivered a plot of lentils.

I also much appreciate the editing labors both of my daughter Corinne—an education major in college—as well as my wife Caroline and her parents.

Prologue

A few notes should be made here in the Prologue to this book. One is that the writer feels his smallness in taking up a subject that pertains to the Nature of God—of course, as revealed in the Bible—and, reflexively, God's view of Man's relationship with Himself.

Fundamentally, this book is written out of a deep and persistent desire to help all of us as Christians to come to a greater understanding of our place eternally in Christ before God.

In respect of this, any reference to "Christian" in this book denotes a true, believing Christian. If there is a reference to an unbeliever (i.e., a professing Christian only) a note will be made to that effect.

So much thanks—more than could be expressed, certainly—are due to the many faithful and ministering Christians who have gone before and "born the burden of the day and the heat" so that we in the early 21st century have the benefit of their spiritual exercises. Of course, we must always "prove the spirits" (1 John 4:1) to ensure that any ministry can bear the heat of the fire (1 Corinthians 3:13); nevertheless, the writer feels the substantial advantage of having been able, at least in part, to draw from wells as to Biblical truths that have been re-dug in recent centuries (Genesis 26:18). Good ministry serves to burnish (never embellish) the Word of God—"If any one speak—as oracles of God; if any one minister—as of strength which God supplies; that God in all things may be glorified through Jesus Christ" (1 Peter 4:11).

I should state in advance that certain scriptures are quoted some number of times—and, truths emphasized and then re-emphasized—throughout the book. This might appear to be an undue repetition; however, it is largely due to a desire to weave certain scriptural precepts throughout the pages of this book. Also, *italicized Scripture verses* are used for my emphasis, and are not present in the original Biblical text.

Lastly, it is to be noted that all scripture quotations are taken from the JN Darby Bible translation due to its exceptional accuracy. This translation can be found online in any number of places—I typically use www.biblegateway.com .

Table of Contents

The Beginning

Almost two thousand years ago the apostle Paul queried, "Even lifeless things giving a sound, whether pipe or harp, if they give not distinction to the sounds, how shall it be known what is piped or harped? For also, if the trumpet give an uncertain sound, who shall prepare himself ...?"

As we read Paul's inspired words in 1 Corinthians 14, the Lord's words in Matthew 5 must also have a particular urgency for all concerned Christians—"Ye are the light of the world: a city situated on the top of a mountain cannot be hid. Nor do [men] light a lamp and put it under the bushel, but upon the lamp-stand, and it shines for all who are in the house. Let your light thus shine before men."

The greatest revelation in scripture is to the existence of and nature of God. In relation to man, there have never been any greater or more vital scriptural truths than those that communicate the elevated place of a race of men created in the image of God. This sublime thread runs throughout the Bible from the early pages of the Book of Genesis to the closing chapter of The Revelation. Christianity, of course, involves God's highest thoughts in relation to man—truths especially pertinent as bearing on Christendom today in the early 21st century. To lack comprehension as to this is to not only reduce the fullness of the Christian relationship with Divine Persons, other Christians and men in general; but, it diminishes, at best, and even skews, at worst, Christian testimony on this earth.

This book, with the gracious help of a Holy God, seeks to draw upon the great truths of Scripture to help every Christian—from the newly converted to those already many years on the Christian path—from the young to the old—from those "weak in the faith" (Roman 14:1) to the veteran pastor or apologist—to be shown afresh the "riches of the glory of this mystery among the nations, which is Christ in you the hope of glory" (Colossians 1:27). Paul highlights in Ephesians 3 "that ye may be *fully* able to apprehend with all the saints what [is] the breadth and length and depth and height; and to know the love of the Christ which surpasses knowledge; that ye may be filled [even] to all the fulness of God." Amen.

It is a vast—and, vastly profound—matter to undertake an exposition from beginning to end of any particular subject in scripture. In respect of the essential subject at hand and to further understand God's ways throughout His creation—and, in particular, His ways with man—we need to highlight various points in a path through scripture. So, while this book is in no way intended to be a mere history of God and His people it is well to reference the beginning.

"In the beginning God created the heavens and the earth" (Genesis 1:1). Several elements are of immediate interest. One is that God appeared, if you will, from a past eternity to create His universe. The eternal and omniscient God is spoken of in the Bible as pre-dating and outside of time and space—"Before the mountains were brought forth, and thou hadst formed the earth and the world, *even from eternity to eternity thou art God*" (Psalm 90:2) and in Exodus 3 He is the great "I AM THAT I AM". In respect of this latter quotation, and as a slight aside, it is of particular enjoyment to a heart engaged with God that in both the Old and New Testaments the Bible sets out a number of names of God—each revealing to us an aspect of His Divinity. In the OT[1] the Hebrew word for Jehovah is *Yahveh* or *Yehveh* which is the ever-existing One. *Elohim* is the plural of *Eloah*—the Supreme—and is defined as Deity in the absolute sense. *El* means the Mighty; *Jah* is the Existing One objectively and *Adonai* is translated Lord. In Isaiah 9:6 we have this: "For unto us a child is born, unto us a son is given; and the government shall be upon his shoulder; and his name is called Wonderful, Counsellor, Mighty God, Father of Eternity, Prince of Peace." Pause and consider—what if, speaking reverently, our wondrous God was known only by one title—God? However blessed that would yet be—is it not of considerably greater import and attraction that this same God reveals himself in the Bible by such distinct, varied and characteristic Names? Such distinctions are evidence of God's desire that we enter into a deeper understanding of Himself, and New Testament revelation regarding the Persons of the Godhead ultimately provide us with the highest and most intimate understanding of Divine Persons.

A second, lateral consideration in relation to Genesis 1:1 is this: What caused the eternal God to move in such a way as to produce creation and, in particular, Man as His creature? As we have in our lovely hymn of some antiquity—"What raised the wondrous thought"?[2] The answer is simple although ineffable—"that I may dwell among them" (Exodus 5:28).

Only a few verses after this initial revelation of God in His creatorial power in Genesis 1:1 is one of the most momentous statements ever uttered in creation—"Come, let us make man in our image, after our likeness." This is subsequent to all the

---

[1] OT means Old Testament; NT means New Testament

[2] (http://www.bible-ministry.com/hymn-92)

scriptural detail of God wonderfully providing a world for the advent of Man—"God himself who formed the earth and made it, he who established it,—not as waste did he create it: *he formed it to be inhabited*" (Isaiah 45:18).

Consider the glory of God's nature in creating this earth to provide a habitation for man. It is neither a small concept nor was it an insignificant execution of God's thoughts. The record of the Holy Spirit is this—"And God saw everything that he had made, and behold it was *very good*." The earth is a vast place, relatively speaking, and almost incalculable in its detail. It was designed in every way by the great Architect to not only sustain life for a myriad of complex and wonderful life forms; but, also to furnish a habitation in which God could provide for and sustain man. The Bible shows that God's thoughts were for the mutuality of a relationship that was, at that point, in a morally unclouded scene. Men speak of paradise; but, reflect on the original Paradise of God—Man and the woman built from his rib (wonderful blessing in itself) set in a splendid sphere in which all was provided and the Lord Himself could visit "in the cool of the day." We can add that Man's only requirement was to hearken to the word of God.

We can contemplate the thoughts of the Lord, reverently speaking, as He fashioned Man out of the moistened dust. God could easily have said, "Let there be Man"; but, His thoughts in affection towards His creature were such that the Lord personally built Man. Here on earth men build and create in an immense variety of ways according to their thoughts and predilections (the first recorded commencement of which—the tower of Babel in Genesis 11—was a concerted effort in independency from God); but, consider the astounding result of the Lord's careful creation of Man. The Psalmist went a step further—he said, "When I see thy heavens, the work of thy fingers, the moon and stars, which thou hast established; What is man, that thou art mindful of him? and the son of man, that thou visitest him? Thou hast made him a little lower than the angels, and hast crowned him with glory and splendour. Thou hast made him to rule over the works of thy hands; thou hast put everything under his feet" (Psalm 8).

God's care and concern for man are evident in virtually every page of scripture. Indeed, the entirety of the Bible has been, we might reverently say, painstakingly selected by God and written at length to inform us as to Who he is, and His thoughts towards, and ways with, man. The Lord said to the religious leaders of the day (John 5:39), "Ye search the scriptures, for ye think that in them ye have life eternal, and they it is which bear witness concerning me." What a generous and loving God we have! Who else could in such detail and yet in such fullness inform man about the practical as well as the moral histories of creation and time. The Bible even leads on ultimately into a future eternity in which all moral issues in the universe will have been fully reconciled to God's satisfaction and He Himself will be "all in all." Thus, we readily understand the apostle Paul's eulogy in Romans 11—"O depth of riches both of [the] wisdom and knowledge of God! how unsearchable his judgments, and untraceable his ways! For who has known [the] mind of [the] Lord, or who has been his counsellor?"

In accord with God's mercy and grace, we see in a review of the moral fall of man in the Garden of Eden that Man did not die immediately. Indeed, Adam lived over 900 years—and the Lord Himself fashioned skins with which to clothe His fallen creature. This, of course, looked on to the redemptive act many centuries later of the very same Lord on the Cross; yet,

17

it speaks to our hearts of the care of God in providing a covering for a creature now fallen from his initial full blessings.

God provides for all men—the Lord said, "your Father who is in [the] heavens; for he makes his sun rise on evil and good, and sends rain on just and unjust" (Matthew 5:45). In the character of the gracious and compassionate God with whom we have to do, it is even set out in Isaiah 28 that His necessary acts of discipline in judgment on this unholy world are "strange" and "unwonted." A brother has written touchingly in his Gospel tract[3], "God's heart is toward men, toward the whole human race, for the gospel is for man universally, yet it is for you particularly. What do we not owe to God? Every heart-beat we owe to Him, and He has been interested in every one of them; but for Him your heart would long ago have stopped its beating! He has surrounded every one of us with the tokens of His mercy, the glorious sun in the heavens, the air, the food; look around your table at meal-time and see the infinite and detailed care of your God!"

We cannot possibly understand the reason for all that God creates unless we understand the Divine Nature of love. We know that some people we meet in this world are almost immediately lovable by nature—why do we take so long to fully and more properly comprehend the nature of God as being love? The very definition of love in the Bible is this: "God is love" (1 John 4:8). The Bible has two absolute and clarion statements as to the nature of God—(1) *God is love* (John 4:8) and (2) *God is light* (1 John 1:5). There are other, similar statements—such as in Psalm 99:9, "Exalt Jehovah our God, and worship at the hill of his holiness; for *holy is Jehovah our*

---

[3] (http://www.bible-ministry.com/gospel-particularly-for-you)

God." However, relative to God's Nature, all of Scripture essentially links back to the two statements listed above.

For many Christians, part of the difficulty, evidently, in fully entering into our Christian heritage and calling can be an innate sluggishness in properly understanding the absolute and essential nature of God as revealed in these and other statements. It is what is indefinite in our minds and hearts as to God that then leads both to a faulty apprehension of Christianity and, similarly, to a more indistinct relationship with God Himself, other Christians and men.

We can, on this subject, best see misapprehensions about God as reflected in the minds of natural men. I recall that, in my late twenties after I had made a necessary and substantial committal to the Lord, a longtime friend with whom I had then shared—perhaps a bit baldly—the Gospel and the change it had effected in my life had sent me a playing-sized card with an illustration of a bearded, robed man and an accompanying message that was something to the effect of "Do not attempt to understand me—just do what I command." This was this friend's mindset as to God—His entire misapprehension was not God's fault, certainly; but, rather, the result of "being darkened in understanding, estranged from the life of God by reason of the ignorance which is in them, by reason of the hardness of their hearts" (Ephesians 4:18). The point I make is that any reduced understanding of God's inherent Nature will of necessity result in a skewed outlook as to Him and His attitude towards, and thus ways with, man.

In the previous paragraph I spoke of what is so often presented as a typical illustration as to the Lord's appearance—robed, bearded and serene. But, it should be of some importance that we understand what the Scripture says as to the appearance and the presence of the Lord when He was here on this earth. Isaiah writes as to the Messiah in chapter 53: "he hath no form nor lordliness, and when we see him, there is no beauty that we should desire him." This is in direct contrast to almost every illustration depicting the Lord in manhood when He was here on earth.

Thus—concerning the Lord's physical appearance and bearing here on this earth almost two thousand years ago—it is evident that the natural mind of man tends toward depicting the Lord in His manhood as having classically smooth and appealing features, and a certain calm but lordly bearing. But, Isaiah shows that He has no natural beauty and no form nor lordliness. Why, you might ask, is this important? Does it change His role as Messiah and as God? Actually, it does. There was evidently no natural/physical appeal to the Lord—that type of appeal is left to the man of sin[4]. There was nothing to attract men outwardly—it was Who He was not how He looked that was an attraction (of course, *that* attraction was due to God's work in the hearts and minds of those so affected). In contrast, we have as to Absalom—King David's son—(a clear type in many ways of the man of sin) this language: "But in all Israel there was none to be so much praised as Absalom for his beauty: from the sole of his foot even to the crown of his head there was no blemish in him. And when he shaved his head (for it was at every year's end that he shaved it, because it was heavy on him, therefore he shaved it), he weighed the hair of his head at two hundred shekels after the king's weight." It is telling that Absalom—evidently a compellingly attractive man naturally—murdered his own brother. When I became a teenager I naively had in mind that pretty girls were, as a result of

---

[4] See 2 Thessalonians 2:3—"the man of sin .... the son of perdition".

their appearance, virtuous girls; but, I found out that physical beauty is no indicator of moral worth.[5]

As a final note, one of the reasons I raised this point as to the appearance of the Lord is that the thrust of this book involves, ultimately, the Christian relationship with Divine Persons *and the great, resultant necessity of being aligned in our hearts and minds as to exactly that which the Holy Spirit sets out in Scripture for our edification.* God does not consider that it is acceptable to have various, diverse beliefs as to Biblical teaching (the apostle Paul writes, for example, in 2 Corinthians 13:11, "For the rest, brethren, rejoice; be perfected; be encouraged; *be of one mind*; be at peace; and the God of love and peace shall be with you."). This matter of depictions of the Lord's appearance may seem to be a trivial question of the truth (and, in one sense, it is trivial); however, it is a casual mindset towards what God sets out in His inspired Word that leads to error in doctrine—and, larger more vital truths can then be negatively affected.

---

[5] Especially in today's society in 2018 where there is such a heightened emphasis on physical appearance, it is well to keep in mind God's estimation of purely natural appeal: "Gracefulness is deceitful, and beauty is vain" (Proverbs 31:30)

Christian Power and Intelligence

Our power as Christians is spiritual—indeed, the very conflict here "is not against blood and flesh, but against principalities, against authorities, against the universal lords of this darkness, *against spiritual [power] of wickedness in the heavenlies*" (Ephesians 6:12). Moses had to learn in chapter 4 of Exodus that his staff upon which he depended naturally was as a serpent, and that his natural heart produced leprosy. It is vital to understand that Christianity is a system centered in Christ and made living and practical through the power of the indwelling Holy Spirit. It has nothing to say, in that respect, to the natural mind of man. In Exodus 5, as already quoted, it was for God to "dwell *among*"; however, in Ephesians 2:22 it is "a habitation of God *in* the Spirit." The Lord informed the woman at the well of Sychar in John 4:24 that "God [is] a spirit; and they who worship him must worship [him] *in spirit and truth*." This leaves no room for the natural man with his independent mind and proclivities which, as Romans 8:6 highlights, is a "mind of death".

In a sense, it is entirely understandable that much of the immediate difficulty for Christians to properly—according to scripture—find our place and calling before God, our relationship to other Christians and our relationship to unbelievers devolves down to being left here, for the present, in bodies of flesh in an earthly setting. Paul writes in 2 Corinthians 4:7, "we have this treasure in earthen vessels"—and therein we suffer a conflict. The "old man" is attracted to all that is around in a world system predicated on the desires and goals of the old man. Why has God left us thus—what is His mind as to this condition?

Paul finishes the same section in 2 Corinthians 4 by saying, "that the surpassingness of the power may be of God, and not from us." The power is there; but, it is from God and not from a reliance on what is natural. God "taketh not pleasure in the legs of a man" (Psalm 147:10) and Zechariah 4:6 states "Not by might, nor by power, *but by my Spirit*." This power from God is to the effect that "If we live by the Spirit, let us walk also by the Spirit" (Galatians 5:25) and, earlier in verse 15, "But I say, Walk in [the] Spirit, and ye shall *no way* fulfil flesh's lust." We see that we have the power to be overcomers. This testimony of the Christian as overcomer is important to Heaven.

The overcomer is especially highlighted in the early chapters of The Revelation, and God's provision for us in our earthly conflict is seen in detail in "the panoply of God" set out by Paul in chapter 6 of Ephesians. We can expand upon this in a later section in this book as it is important to understand that Christianity inherently is not *attainment*; but, rather, *endowment*. This is to say that God both imparts to us a new and necessary nature through new birth and also that we have an associated, innate power through the indwelling Holy Spirit ("Ye are of God, children, and have overcome them, because *greater is he that [is] in you than he that [is] in the world*—1 John 4:4).

Of course, in Philippians 3:16 Paul writes, "But whereto we have *attained*, [let us] walk in the same steps"; but, this is the practical effect of righteousness through faith which is the primary teaching of the chapter. It is the difference between attempting to climb the mountain in contrast to being set upon

23

the mountaintop and needing, in a sense, only to maintain that elevated position. My Dad used to say, "We are given everything by God at the outset—we then need to work it out in our practical circumstances here on earth." We see this in God telling the Israelites that all of the promised land had been given to them; but, that they needed to take possession and make it a practical reality—"Every place whereon the sole of your foot shall tread shall be yours" (Deuteronomy 11:24).

Commencing in Genesis, and moving through scripture we see that God is constantly accounting for and providing for His creature. Even with Cain—a man so clearly a murderer— God accedes to Cain's statement that "My punishment is too great to be borne" (Genesis 4:13) and puts a mark on him that not only would no other slay him but, if they did so, he would be revenged seven-fold ("vengeance is mine, saith the Lord"— Deuteronomy 32:35). When Moses sought to see the Lord's glory, the Lord passed graciously before him saying, "Jehovah, Jehovah God merciful and gracious, slow to anger, and abundant in goodness and truth" (Exodus 34:6), and covered him in the cleft of the rock. "Rock of ages ... cleft for me" is our well-known hymn, and the Lord's glory was seen from behind—amazing reality when we consider that God dwells in light unapproachable. How well we can harmonize in acknowledging, "O merciful and gracious God"!

It also does us well to remember that, in this context of considering God's longsuffering ways with man (2 Peter 3:9), sin is entirely abhorrent to God. It says in Habakkuk 1:13 that the Lord is "of purer eyes than to behold evil, and canst not look on mischief" and that early on in Genesis 6 when the Lord saw that "the wickedness of Man was great on the earth .... He repented that he had made Man on the earth, and it grieved him in his heart." We can be perhaps a bit casual in our minds as

24

to the character of sin; but, I repeat, sin is abhorrent to God. And yet, not only has God never destroyed Man[6]; but, instead, He has made every effort, reverently speaking, to ensure that Man is saved. The prophet Ezekiel said many centuries ago, "As I live, saith the Lord Jehovah, I have no pleasure in the death of the wicked; but that the wicked turn from his way and live. Turn ye, turn ye from your evil ways; for why will ye die" (Ezekiel 33:11).

Ezekiel's statements link in a wonderful way with the Lord's words in the well-known verse of John 3:16—"For God so loved the world, that he gave his only-begotten Son, that whosoever believes on him may not perish, but have life eternal"— and it does well to pause here so as to state a clarion principle to aid in understanding the Bible. This statement can be simply put as this: God never changes and as a result Divine principles never change. This can be readily seen in the Lord's words through the prophet Malachi, "For I Jehovah change not." This is definitive. This statement is mirrored by another, almost identical statement made as to the Lord in Hebrews 13—"Jesus Christ [is] the same yesterday, and to-day, and to the ages [to come]." And, of course, there are other, similar statements to which we could allude.

It is vital to recognize this simple but cogent fact as to Divine unchangeableness. If the Lord (who is God Himself, of course) never changes this means that the moral character in which He approaches men never changes. Thus, the Divine *principles* of the Old Testament are the same principles we see

---

[6] We see that, even in relation to the Flood in the time of Noah, that "the longsuffering of God waited in [the] days of Noah while the ark was preparing" (1 Peter 3:20)

expressed in the New Testament. This comprehension makes it easier to understand and link both the Old and the New—and, we should, as Christians, be well able to express the precepts and doctrine of the entire Bible ("Have an outline of sound words"—2 Timothy 1:13). Thus, the Lord says in Matthew 13:52, "For this reason every scribe discipled to the kingdom of the heavens is like a man [that is] a householder who brings out of his treasure things *new* and *old*." We must notice that the "new" is first—i.e., the Old Testament is properly understood in the light of the New Testament, and so we have therefore the "type" (*tupos* in the Greek) of the OT and the anti-type (*antitupos*) in the New Testament (see Paul's words in 1 Corinthians 10:6 as to "types").

So, for Christians the OT can sometimes appear to be a bit of a puzzle—especially in relation to the tabernacle system as provided through Moses. But, in Exodus 25 the Lord said that He was giving to Moses a *pattern*. The mirror statement to this in the New Testament is seen in Hebrews 8:5 as the apostle relates the priests' place in the OT, "who serve the *representation and shadow* of heavenly things, according as Moses was oracularly told [when] about to make the tabernacle; for See, saith He, that thou make all things according to the *pattern* which has been shewn to thee in the mountain." The earthly pattern was a representation of heavenly things. In the OT Israel is viewed as God's earthly people—every man under his vine and under his fig tree (1 Kings 4:25)[7]. When

---

[7] Of course, through redemption, the heavenly side was ultimately in view for the pious Israelite—Hebrews 11 shows that "All these died in faith, not having received the promises, but having seen them from afar off and embraced [them], and confessed that they were strangers and sojourners on the earth. For they who say such things shew clearly that they seek [their] country. And if they had called to mind that from whence they

we come to the NT it is "in my Father's house [i.e., in Heaven] there are many abodes .... for I go to prepare you a place" (John 14:2). Christians are shown to have a heavenly inheritance,—Israel an earthly inheritance. This is a huge distinction. An earthly people is blessed by God on earth (see Deuteronomy 28—the blessings enumerated there for Israel are shown to be entirely earthly) whereas for the Christian we see in Ephesians 1:3, "Blessed [be] the God and Father of our Lord Jesus Christ, who has blessed us with every spiritual blessing *in the heavenlies* in Christ".

One is presented essentially as an earthly people with earthly blessings; the other a heavenly people on earth. If I spoke to you about a Sicilian man whose family lineage goes back a century in Sicily—that person is truly a Sicilian. If, on the other hand, I present you with an Englishman who is currently residing in Sicily—is this latter man a Sicilian simply because he is living in Sicily? Obviously not; yet, Christians move through "this present evil world" (Galatians 1:4) as if they belong here when, instead, their heritage is heavenly. The Lord says succinctly in John 15:19, "*ye are not of the world*, but I have chosen you out of the world." Not recognizing the nature of our heavenly calling while yet on earth ("the first man out of [the] earth, made of dust; the second man, out of heaven"—1 Corinthians 15) is a misapprehension as to the vital and fundamental reality of the Christian calling. This misapprehension considerably clouds Christian testimony. Of course, it is important to state here that we do not want to drift into a line of mystical thinking as to our current Christian

---

went out, they had had opportunity to have returned; but now they seek a better, that is, *a heavenly*".

estate—we certainly are squarely here on the earth; *but, it is not our home nor our calling.*

It should be of concern to any honest and exercised Christian—and, this book is written in view of honest and concerned Christian appraisal—that in the first chapter in the book of The Revelation the Lord is seen walking among the seven lamps (the chapter shows that "the seven lamps are seven assemblies"). But, in the very next chapter He speaks to Ephesus as to removing the lamp out of its place unless they repented as to how they had fallen. In all the following addresses to the next six assemblies the lamp is no longer seen! Why is this? Paul wrote in Philippians 2 "that ye may be harmless and simple, irreproachable children of God in the midst of a crooked and perverted generation; *among whom ye appear as lights[8] in [the] world*, holding forth [the] word of life". Yet, the Holy Spirit records in Revelation that according to God's estimation the lamps/lights are no longer seen. Is this not concerning? Who is to blame? You and I! We know that in scripture gold is typically used to represent what pertains to the Divine Nature (the temple built by Solomon was entirely overlaid within and without with gold). Even those many centuries ago as a result of the same type of declension that the Church now suffers, Jeremiah weepingly records, "how is the gold become dim!" (Lamentations 4:1). We can readily see today in glancing around Christendom that the Church's ability to reflect[9] the nature of God has dimmed.

As we continue to move towards the main thrust of this book there are yet other points to notice before we get there, and I

---

[8] Notice that it is "lights" spoken of here—i.e., the individual side

[9] See Genesis 1:14-18—the great and the small lights

can say that I never tire in taking up "the words of life eternal" (John 6:68) that characterize the Bible. The apostle John records in his first epistle, "That which was from [the] beginning, that which we have heard, which we have seen with our eyes; that which we contemplated, and our hands handled, *concerning the word of life*". Will it not be lovely indeed to actually see the Lord's blessed face and to hear words spoken directly by Him in our Heavenly home? And that for all eternity! As Paul writes in 1 Corinthians 2:9, "Things which eye has not seen, and ear not heard, and which have not come into man's heart, which God has prepared for them that love him, but God has revealed to us by [his] Spirit." Amen.

We have, in this respect, this beautiful hymn:[10]

> LORD, in Thee we taste the sweetness
>
> Of the Tree of Life above;
>
> Taste its own eternal meetness
>
> For the heav'nly land we love.
>
> In eternal counsels purposed,
>
> Food of heav'nly life to be;
>
> Fresh and ever new are yielded
>
> Fruits of life on that blest Tree.

---

[10] http://www.bible-ministry.com/hymn-7

Varied fruits of richest flavour
Offers still the Tree divine;
One itself, the same for ever,
Every precious fruit is Thine.

Fruits that now our souls have tasted
By the Spirit from above,
While through desert lands we've hasted;
Fruits of perfect, endless love.

The Church—the Pillar and Base of the Truth

In respect to what has been said about the Divine expectation that the Church[11] is be a light upon the mountaintop, it should profoundly resonate with every exercised Christian that the Church is "[the] assembly of [the] living God, [the] pillar and base of the truth" (1 Timothy 3:15). Is this not compelling language? The Lord is said to be "the way, *the truth* and the life" and here we have the Church spoken of as the *pillar and base of the truth.* Scripture presents that in Christ and His Church are displayed God's greatest thoughts. In Solomon's temple

---

[11] We understand as Christians that the true Church—better translated according to the original as "Assembly" which means a "calling out" (i.e., a separation of a people to a Holy God)—is composed only of true believing Christians. At the present, however, viewed in Scripture as the "great house", the public body includes professing Christians. For this reason some refer to the "invisible" and the "visible" Church in hope of elucidating that the true Church is a spiritual entity (entirely true) that cannot be understood by the natural mind (also true) which is, therefore, "invisible"; whereas the public body—due to the admixture—is the visible entity. However, to adopt such language is to fall into a trap of Satan, because then the premise is that there cannot be an adequate evidence of the "real" Church in this world; however, the Lord's words are in diametric opposition to this notion as He says in Matthew 5 not only that "Ye are the light of the world" but "Let your light thus shine upon men"—an active reality. The query might be raised as to how this comports with the aforementioned scripture in Revelation showing that the lampstand is publicly removed; however, the underlying desire in writing this book is to help us all as Christians to understand that the public failures in Christendom are in no way to affect either Divine principles nor our individual faithfulness to the same, unchanging principles. This is seen with Joshua who said, "choose you this day whom ye will serve .... but as for me and my house we will serve Jehovah" (Joshua 24:15).

there were two majestic pillars for the porch made of molten brass (representing solidity)—the name of the one was Jachin and the name of the other Boaz. Paul writes to the Corinthians regarding the Church in its heavenly place, "Do ye not then know that the saints shall judge the world? and if the world is judged by you, are ye unworthy of [the] smallest judgments? Do ye not know that we shall judge angels? and not then matters of this life?" (1 Corinthians 6:2).

The Bible rests upon the foundation of the grace and love of God; however, the backdrop is His judgment of all things as to right or wrong. Isaiah 61:8 shows that, "For I, Jehovah, love judgment." *Right judgment corroborates and maintains the truth.* Grace and truth are linked in scripture—"For the law was given by Moses: *grace and truth* subsists through Jesus Christ" (John 1:17). Many Christians have a substantial misapprehension as to the nature of judgment. We all make judgments all day every day as to what is right and helpful even in common matters of life here. Are we then to cease judgment when it comes to moral issues—especially concerning the house of God? The Psalmist says (Psalm 89), "*Righteousness and judgment* are the foundation of thy throne; loving-kindness and truth go before thy face." Christianity cannot exist and function without proper judgments about everything—judgments that are to mirror the judgments of God Himself.

The difficulty is perhaps partially due to some misapplying certain scriptures—such as that of Matthew 7: "Judge not, that ye may not be judged; for with what judgment ye judge, ye shall be judged; and with what measure ye mete, it shall be measured to you." It is well to understand that the Greek word here translated as "judge" carries the meaning of "condemn" or "sentence to". We cannot, as we see in this scripture, assign a sentence of condemnation to others—i.e., "You did thus and so and as a result this or that is or will be your punishment." God alone passes final judgment.

However, it is not only scriptural but mandatory that righteous judgments be made by Christians in order to maintain the moral stature of Christian relationships with each other and with God Himself. The Lord says in John 7:24, "judge righteous judgment." It does well to consider Matthew 18 in this respect: "But if thy brother sin against thee, go, reprove him between thee and him alone. If he hear thee, thou hast gained thy brother. But if he do not hear [thee], take with thee one or two besides, that every matter may stand upon the word of two witnesses or of three. But if he will not listen to them, tell it to the assembly; and if also he will not listen to the assembly, let him be to thee as one of the nations and a tax-gatherer. Verily I say to you, Whatsoever ye shall bind on the earth shall be bound in heaven."

There can be no gainsaying that this scripture distinctly sets out the need for (and, just as importantly, the manner of) judgment in relation to Christian fellowship. It is not here an arbitrary judgment; but, rather, a judgment entirely according to scripture so as to maintain the holiness of Christian relationships and, by extension, the holiness due to God's house. Matthew 18 is not optional—it is required! I say strongly that the notion with many Christians of not judging is a beguilement of Satan. When Ananias and Sapphira sought to dissemble in Acts 5 as to the price for which they had sold the estate, Peter did not say, "Oh it is a small matter and besides I can't judge them—I have to leave this entirely to God." No! He said, "why has Satan filled thy heart that thou shouldest lie to the Holy Spirit" (Acts 5:3). It is a major point to understand that the Holy Spirit indwells God's house, and Acts 5:3 shows that God wants everything open and judged.[12]

Furthermore, the scripture about judgment in Matthew 7 to which we have already alluded concludes with this statement—very often, perhaps, ignored and overlooked: "cast out first the beam out of thine eye, and *then thou wilt see clearly to cast out the mote out of the eye of thy brother.*" Thus, we see that this section in Matthew 7 does not set aside judgment—rather, it reinforces that judgment should take place; but, in a scriptural way. The point here is that we start with judgment as to our own selves; then we are able to help in matters of judgment pertaining to other circumstances. The principle is seen in Ezekiel 9 where judgment is to "begin at my sanctuary."

In the most emphatic way, the entire foundation of the Cross of Christ involves the judgment of God against sin and a sinful, fallen world. The Lord said, "Now is the judgment of this world" (John 12:31). Are Christians then to enter blithely into Christianity and to forego judgments against what is wrong? Who might be behind the notion that righteous judgment is unscriptural? Is it the same deceiver who suggested to Eve that she and Adam would "certainly not die" if they contravened the Lord's words about eating of the tree of the knowledge of good and evil? The Lord's own words as quoted in John 7 are, "Judge not according to sight, but *judge righteous judgment*"—nothing could be plainer than this. A Christian who has been properly converted—a Christian who is fully led by the Holy Spirit—a Christian who loves the Lord and the

---

[12] See, also, in this respect, Mark 11:16—"and suffered not that any one should carry any *package* through the temple", and, also, The Revelation 4:6—"before the throne, as a glass sea, like crystal" indicating that the ground on which one stands is transparent (i.e., nothing hidden)

saints—a Christian who understands the inviolate nature of God Himself—is then a Christian who stands as one who is constitutionally self-judged and always amenable to being judged. Such a Christian is always ready to apply the "washing of the water of the word" (Ephesians 5:26) to his or her personal circumstances as well as to the moral conditions and the fellowship of others with whom he or she walks. If any think that the intrinsic nature of Christianity is designed to refuse righteous, scriptural judgments and exhortations—such persons are believing a subtle but powerful delusion of Satan. Scripture self-defines itself in respect of the principle of judgment—2 Timothy 3:16 says, "Every scripture [is] divinely inspired, and profitable for teaching, for conviction, for correction, for instruction in righteousness".

The sacrificial system in the Old Testament is not a focus of this section; but, it is still a considerable help to understand these sacrificial types. The sin offering, for example, was to be entirely burned up. What is the meaning of this? It is the "old man" *fully removed* in the Cross of Christ. How is it possible to consider that, if God shows this complete immolation of the old man, the nature of this fallen and condemned creature is to be allowed *any* say or sway in the Divine realm? It is the "little foxes, that spoil the vineyards" (Song of Solomon 2:15). In Leviticus 8, in which the Divine instructions regarding the sin offering and the burnt offering were set out, it is instructive that the innards of the sin offering were to be removed and burned up separately. God was illustrating that what might promote the old man in his inward impulses be definitively eradicated. The burnt offering was also totally burned up; and, it is noteworthy, again, that the internal organs and the fat were—although also burned up—treated separately (i.e., particular attention was to be given to the inward side— a type of our inward thoughts and motivations). In this case of the burnt offering the inwards and the legs were washed with water—a type of the sanctifying attributes of the Word of God as applied to us inwardly. Are these not shown as types of judgment—speaking to the removal of what is not suitable to the holy presence of God? These sacrifices are burned up— they are gone—nothing is left. Christians are to apply the same principles in Christianity—nothing of the corrupt old man is be tolerated (Ephesians 4:22).

The Church cannot properly enter into its character as being the "pillar and base of the truth" (1 Timothy 3:15) without the understanding of the principle of judgment. We do not have to fear as to the demise of the Church, since the Lord said, "I will build my assembly, and hades' gates shall not prevail against it" (Matthew 16:18); however, it is still instructive that, through a lack of proper judgment in Israel, Solomon's temple was destroyed and the two brazen pillars were broken up (see Jeremiah 52).

Christianity—God's Greatest Design

We have shown in this book that God created this world to be inhabited, and created Man "in His image" in view of a relationship with Man. We have considered that Man, commencing with the fall in the Garden of Eden and continuing down through every century, has transgressed against, and failed in every aspect of that which God has so generously provided.

We have seen already that Man naturally, through his sinful estate, is at a hopeless moral distance from a holy God. Paul writes that the natural man is "having no hope, and without God in the world" (Ephesians 2:12). Yet, knowing this, we can thank God for His great mercies and love, as Paul could also write, "for we being still without strength, in [the] due time Christ has died for [the] ungodly" (Romans 5:6). We have seen that God has been infinitely patient and gracious in faithful pursuit of His desire that "all men be saved" (1 Timothy 2:4). We have shown that Christianity is a spiritual system, and that God is unchangeable—providing a firm anchor for faith. We have read that "Righteousness and judgment are the foundation of thy throne" (Psalm 89:14) and that it is an unacceptable delusion that Christians not be in agreement with, and constantly judging, everything and everyone with the same judgments that God judges[13]—otherwise, the practical day-to-day value of the Cross is lost. In short, we have touched upon a number of important points in the understanding of God in His moral Nature and outlook, and, accordingly, our place before Him as men—and, we could have,

---

[13] "Yea, Lord God Almighty, true and righteous [are] thy judgments" (Revelation16:7)—this is the Christian's place—affirmation of God's judgments and precepts

on these points, referred to many other scriptures and related doctrinal precepts.

However, we can now approach the main thrust of this document—and it involves this: What is the nature and constitution of this Christian system, speaking reverently, in which men are brought to God Himself in the power and reality of eternal life, and how does this Christian system work and function on this earth (and, ultimately, in eternity)? This is to say—how does the Bible explain God, Man, sin, salvation and eternity so that Christians can properly answer to all that God has in mind?

It is certainly more than apparent that God is holy and without sin—"And this is the message which we have heard from him, and declare to you, that God is light, and in him is no darkness at all" (1 John 1:5). It is just as apparent that man—God's creature—is by his fallen nature at an immeasurable moral distance from a righteous God. Indeed, the extent of the distance is essentially to be understood in the fact that it was God Himself as "manifest in flesh" (1 Timothy 3:16) who had to come to this earth, and Christ—as Son of God and Son of Man—was lifted up on the Cross in atoning power to remove such moral darkness and distance. No one else could accomplish this incredible redemption. From the simplest perspective it is, in a sense, almost inconceivable that, after the fall of Man in the Garden of Eden, God could and would undertake to bear with man week after month after decade after century in the face of man's innate independency from and rejection of Himself. No mere man would ever put up with such contrariety—it is a glorious testimony to God's long-suffering nature.

And so, one of the most immediate statements to be made about God's implementation of Christianity is that God will not be deterred in anything He undertakes. Paul writes in Romans 8, "For I am persuaded that neither death, nor life, nor angels, nor principalities, nor things present, nor things to come, nor powers, nor height, nor depth, nor any other creature, shall be able to separate us from the love of God, which [is] in Christ Jesus our Lord."

This is a great joy because it helps us to be peaceful in the clamor and chaos of the world around us. Nothing is going to prevent God from effectuating His great thoughts as to redemption for men and ultimately, if we can be permitted leeway in using this phrase, as to the redemption of His creation (see 2 Peter 3:13—"But, according to his promise, we wait for new heavens and a new earth, wherein dwells righteousness").

When the Lord set up the Mosaic system the Bible shows that there were no illusions, reverently speaking, that Man would be able to keep the law. Indeed, the scripture says the exact opposite: "Wherefore by works of law no flesh shall be justified before him; for by law [is] knowledge of sin" (Romans 3:20). The ultimate purpose of the law was to highlight the nature of man's sinful estate—"So that the law indeed [is] holy, and the commandment holy, and just, and good. Did then that which is good become death to me? Far be the thought. *But sin, that it might appear sin,* working death to me by that which is good; in order that sin by the commandment might become exceeding sinful" (Romans 7:12-13).

Nevertheless, God brought in the law to provide a just, right and honorable standard by which man could be measured. As stated, man could not keep the standard and the law served to accentuate man's sinful estate. But, there was another facet to the law. No person could, on a day of judgment, complain to God that he or she had never been given a formal opportunity, so to speak, to prove their righteousness. The word given to Moses was that, if the law was kept, the man could live (Deuteronomy 8:1)—conversely, if a man failed in even one point of the law he was guilty of the entire law (i.e., one sin showed a wholly sinful estate—see James 2:10).

Lastly, we know that there was, indeed, one Man who walked on this earth who could and did keep the law—one Man who was and is entirely without sin (see Hebrews 4:15)—the Man Christ Jesus. This understanding is vital since God has displayed through Christ that a Man not only could but did keep the law; but, in a sense even more exemplary, that "he hath magnified the law, and made it honourable" (Isaiah 42:21). Does not the heart of all the redeemed rejoice in such a One? We shall bear that image—"And as we have borne the image of the [one] made of dust, we shall bear also the image of the heavenly [one]"—1 Corinthians 49! The Lord said in John 8, "Your father Abraham *exulted* in that he should see my day, and he saw and *rejoiced*." Our hearts' rejoicings in the Lord can surely be mirrored by what we see in Psalm 150:

Hallelujah! Praise God in his sanctuary; praise him in the firmament of his power.

Praise him in his mighty acts; praise him according to the abundance of his greatness.

Praise him with the sound of the trumpet; praise him with lute and harp;

Praise him with the tambour and dance; praise him with stringed instruments and the pipe;

Praise him with loud cymbals; praise him
with high sounding cymbals.

Let everything that hath breath praise Jah.
Hallelujah!

Having spoken of the law, it is, of course, vital that we understand the Bible's definition of sin. If we do not understand
God's definition of sin how can we properly ascertain as to
what constitutes sin while we are here in this sinful world? If
a hundred Christians were asked as to the definition of sin,
might we get a variety of answers?

We see that the proper definition is in 1 John 3:4: "sin is lawlessness." The King James Bible, for example, translates this
section, "sin is the transgression of the law". The note given
in the JN Darby translation as to the correct rendering is helpful: "To translate this `sin is the transgression of the law' is
wrong, and gives a false definition of sin, for sin was in the
world, and death as a consequence, before the giving of *the*
law. The Greek reads `sin is lawlessness,' that is, the absence
of the *principle* of the law (not *the* law), or, in other words, of
the control of God over the soul."

This simple difference in Biblical translation and understanding can thus result in a prodigious difference in the way we
make necessary moral estimations as to the actions of ourselves and others. While all judgments have to comport with
scripture, it is evident that, although the law highlights certain
specific sins, the nature of man's sinful state is revealed in ac-
tivities that can be beyond the immediate words of the essential ten commandments. The ultimate reality is that man's
fallen *nature* is lawless—that is to say, it pursues its own desires independent from the authority of God. This helps

41

enormously in clarifying why the old man had to be removed *en toto* on the Cross of Christ—the *nature* is simply incorrigible. Thus, in Romans 7:18 the apostle wrote, "For I know that in me, that is, in my flesh, *good does not dwell.*" This is also why the Lord spoke in a parable in Mark 2 that new wine can only be put into new skins—i.e., new birth (the new skins) is a necessity in order to being brought properly into God's presence. The old man/skins is not suitable—those skins are burst and the wine poured out. Many Christians try to work out their lives here by laboring under the attempt of trying to retain the old skins—or, features of the old skins—to accomodate the new wine. But, that's not Christianity.

Thus, we are shown VERY early in scripture (Genesis 6) that "God said to Noah, The end of all flesh is come before me." This statement is not casual—it carries a moral import far beyond what was then the impending flood. Many centuries later the Holy Spirit records the same principle in its full moral import: "But this I say, brethren, that flesh and blood cannot inherit God's kingdom, nor does corruption inherit incorruptibility" (1 Corinthians 15:50). We have to be born again—to have a different—a new—nature so as to be suitable for the spiritual realm into which God brings us as Christians. It is impossible to emphasize enough that the old man is to be put off and the new man to be put on "which according to God is created in truthful righteousness and holiness" (Ephesians 4:24). Paul writes in 2 Corinthians 5:17, "So if any one [be] in Christ, [*there is*] *a new creation*; the old things have passed away; behold all things have become new."

The misapprehension (or simple refusal) of God's judgment of the old nature—and God's total removal of it—in the Cross of Christ is what leads to the attempt to implement natural thoughts into Christianity. The old man is always ready to assert its own mind and will in the life of the Christian—which is why its total removal in the death of the Cross is necessary to then being able to walk in the "newness of life" (Romans 6:4). The book of Romans sets out the "mechanics", if you will, whereby the Christian can successfully be set free from the hindrances of the old man. Paul shows the moral conflict of this in chapter 7—"for not what I will, this I do; but what I hate, this I practise." This is the place and portion of many Christians—laboring to be righteous—as they wend their way through the week, and many pastors and teachers who are suffering under the same incubus are of little help in their preaching and sermons.

What is the answer to this foundational issue? At the conclusion of Romans 7 Paul cries out, "O wretched man that I [am]! *who shall deliver me* out of this body of death?" The brother felt his own inabilities in his attempts to control the nature and the influences of the old man—influences that, as already noted earlier in this book, involve "the mind of death" (see Romans 8:6)—he lamented that he was, in effect, trapped "in himself". What was the answer to what was naturally an insurmountable dilemma? The need is for *deliverance*—Paul had cried out, "who shall *deliver* me"? The answer is found in the next sentence. Paul writes, "I thank God, *through* Jesus Christ our Lord." The power for deliverance is through Christ personally based on His fully effectuated work on the Cross.

It has been said that a Christian cannot effectively proceed an inch up the Christian path here without the understanding of and the very real effect of deliverance. We can certainly understand the application of the word `deliverance' in practical circumstances. The dictionary defines `deliverance' as "the act of being set free." Paul wrote to Timothy that he had been "delivered out of the lion's mouth" (2 Timothy 4:17)—that is, the Lord had delivered him out of the power of Satan which

43

might have been enacted through Caesar in Rome when Paul was brought in bonds before him (see Acts 25:12). There was written quite some years ago a brief but seminal work on deliverance and I urge you to read it—it will take but a few minutes.[14]

Here is an excerpt from the beginning of this address on deliverance:

> *Answer.* Yes; it is like the prodigal son, he was all right with his father, when his father was on his neck; there was peace, but there was not happiness yet, for he did not feel fit for his father. He said, " I have sinned against heaven, and in thy sight." Have you not found persons who have peace with God, who yet have not happiness because they get very distressed about their own sinfulness?
>
> *Remark.* Would not peace and happiness go together ?
>
> *Answer.* They ought, but they often do not. I think hundreds of persons have peace, who have not happiness; they know it is all right between themselves and God, but they are not at the Supper yet. Why? Because they have not on the best robe. The best robe is Christ. It was the father's answer to the prodigal's utterance of unworthiness.

---

[14] Here is a link: http://www.bible-ministry.com/exegetical-peace-and-deliverance

> JB Stoney, "Peace and Deliverance", John 3:14-15; 4:14, New Series, Volume 6, pgs. 357-365, Cooper & Budd, Ltd., London 1964

Deliverance simply entails two primary aspects in its practical application: (1) the Christian understands and sees that the old man of sin has been removed *from the eye of God* through the redemptive work of Christ and (2) and that, for himself or herself—as a practical consequence through new birth and the indwelling presence and power of the Holy Spirit—the Christian also comprehends fully that the old man is *gone. It has been replaced by a new nature.* A feeble analogy would be like someone (the saved but undelivered Christian) seeking to *control* their diabetes through diet compared to someone (the delivered Christian) who *no longer has* diabetes. Paul's words at the end of chapter 7 of Romans show how deliverance is accomplished—"I thank God, *through*[15] Jesus Christ our Lord"—and those words are then immediately followed by this language in the first two verses of chapter 8: "[There is] then now no condemnation to those in Christ Jesus. *For the law of the Spirit of life in Christ Jesus has set me free from the law of sin and of death.*

This is deliverance. It is the result of the removal of the old man through the implementation of the Cross, and the old man's replacement with a new nature through new birth and the transcendent power and place of the indwelling Holy Spirit. Of course, it is important to state—lest we adopt some

---

[15] i.e., *through* the power of all that the Lord has effectuated on the Cross—including, as a result, the indwelling presence and power of the blessed Holy Spirit

type of mystical apprehension as to the nature of Christianity on this earth—that the old man is still present. John writes, "If we say that we have no sin, we deceive ourselves, and the truth is not in us" (1 John 1:8). Sin is obviously the result of the activity of the old man—the natural mind. So, this last scripture may make the foregoing statements sound a bit like a contradiction; however, they are certainly not a contradiction. They are simply two aspects of the truth. We have to be able to balance scripture—and the point being made as to deliverance is all-important. The practical application of deliverance is akin, in a sense, to deleting a file on a hard drive—it is still on the hard drive but, unless we access it, it is the same as if it no longer exists. God is supplanting the old, fallen nature with a new creation. We see in the OT that the name Jacob means "supplanter"—Jacob supplanted Esau (see Genesis 25:26 and 27:36) and Romans 9:13 shows that God loved the supplanting of Jacob and hated the unspiritual Esau. Strong language!

As set out in the Bible our power for deliverance is centered in Christ, and made effective through the eternal, indwelling power of the Holy Spirit. The Lord said in John 14 that the Holy Spirit will be "with you *forever*." Some think that when Christians get to Heaven since they will be like the Lord (1 John 3:2) there will be either no need for—or, only some sort of quasi-need for—the Holy Spirit. However, this is definitively wrong, as the Lord's words above so clearly illustrate. We cannot do without the Holy Spirit since it is through Him that we have "become partakers of the divine nature" (2 Peter 1:4)—one of the single most transcendent of all scriptural truths).

The Holy Spirit's Presence

We have now come to two fundamental, intertwined truths. The first is that the Lord is clearly not here on the earth – having ascended prior to the day of Pentecost.

The second truth – prophetically foretold in Joel 2:28 and as to which the Lord discoursed in John 16 – is the advent of the Holy Spirit. The Lord was careful at that time to distinctly highlight these two truths: "I did not say these things unto you from [the] beginning, because I was with you. *But now I go to him that has sent me*, and none of you demands of me, Where goest thou? But because I have spoken these things to you, sorrow has filled your heart. But I say the truth to you, It is profitable for you that I go away; for if I do not go away, the Comforter will not come to you; *but if I go I will send him to you."*

When the Lord was here He explained to and taught His disciples concerning the kingdom of the heavens—the spiritual realm into which the Christian is brought. He said to them, "Because to you it is given to know the mysteries of the kingdom of the heavens, but to them it is not given." However, it is abundantly clear from scripture that the Lord is now no longer here on this earth. "Now a summary of the things of which we are speaking [is], We have such a one high priest *who has sat down on [the] right hand of the throne of the greatness in the heavens*" (Hebrews 1:8). Who, then, shall teach us here on earth?

John 16:13 gives us the answer in the Lord's own words, "But when he is come, the Spirit of truth, *he shall guide you into all the truth*". How important, then, is the indwelling place of the Holy Spirit? Romans 8 shows that "they that are in flesh cannot please God. But ye are not in flesh but in Spirit, if indeed God's Spirit dwell in you; but *if any one has not [the] Spirit of Christ he is not of him.*" However, we are concerned now with the practical effect of the Holy Spirit as indwelling the believer. The Lord said in John 16:13 "But when he is come, the Spirit of truth, *he shall guide you into all the truth*". We must notice the phrase "<u>all</u> the truth." Pilate said, "What is truth?"; but, we know that Jesus Christ is "the way, the truth, and the life." Here, then, is a cardinal/vital statement—*the Holy Spirit always leads the Christian to what is of God and centered in Christ.* The Lord said, "He shall glorify me, for he shall receive of mine and shall announce [it] to you" (John 16:14).

The simple reality is that we cannot navigate, speaking reverently, in the realm of what is Divine if we do not have the indwelling presence *and the lead* of the Holy Spirit. The prophet Isaiah says in chapter 30, "And when ye turn to the right hand or when ye turn to the left, thine ears shall hear a word behind thee, saying, This is the way, walk ye in it." We can see from Isaiah 30 and John 16 that the Holy Spirit is the indwelling Guide for the Christian. Of course, "God is one" (1 Timothy 2:5) and the Lord speaks extensively in John 14 as to the unity of the Godhead in respect of the believer being indwelt; however, we must distinguish between the abstract and the practical in that the Bible is explicit that the Lord has ascended to Heaven to prepare us a place, has sat down at the right hand of God the Father, and has sent the Holy Spirit to indwell the believer.

This following hymn writer well understood the blessed place and service of the Holy Spirit:

> Holy Spirit, gift divine,
>
> Praise and thanks be ever Thine;
>
> Thou dost guide us here below,
>
> Christ, our life, through Thee we know.
>
> What a joy it is to be,
>
> Blessed Spirit, here with Thee!
>
> As to follow Thee we learn,
>
> So Thy wisdom we discern;
>
> Thou dost all our journey through
>
> Teach us what to say and do;
>
> To our minds the thoughts divine
>
> Clear and plain before us shine.
>
> Holy Spirit, Thee we bless;
>
> Comforter Thou art to us!
>
> Death o'ershadows all the scene,
>
> But on Thy support we lean.
>
> Thou dost bring the glory nigh,

Help our faith to look on high.

All that Christ in love has giv'n,

All the Father's wealth from heav'n,

Richly through Thy service flow;

Help divine through Thee we know.

Leader, Thou, the desert through—

Thanks to Thee is ever due!

At this point I should like to pause and incorporate something written quite some years ago; but, which is blessed as to the place of the Holy Spirit as seen in relation to the Lord's path when here. The Lord is ever unique, of course, but, this following extract is especially endearing as it looks on to our primary subject in this book—the place of the indwelling Holy Spirit in the believer's path here. Here it is:

> With regard to the expression, "the Spirit of holiness," I would notice that the Holy Spirit is, so to speak, the operative power in the resurrection as in everything that God has created or done. Thus Peter says, with regard to the Lord's resurrection, "Put to death in the flesh, but quickened by the Spirit " (1 Peter 3:18); and of the believer it is said, "But if the Spirit of him that

raised up Jesus from the dead dwell in you, he that raised up Christ from the dead shall also quicken your mortal bodies by his Spirit that dwelleth in you," Rom. 8:11.

But why is it spoken of as "according to the Spirit of holiness"? Because the Holy Spirit is, as it were, the operative power of God for producing in man all that is well-pleasing to Him. This power is, of course, always in God. By it He created the world; by it He wrought in the instruments of the Old Testament and in the prophets. But now He had been acting in the human life of Christ, and in the production of the new form of humanity, according to this divine power. But Christ as Man was *born* of the Holy Spirit; His life, though human in every respect[16], was the expression of the power of the Holy Spirit. He cast out devils by the Holy Spirit. His words were spirit and life. The fulness of the Godhead dwelt in Him bodily, but His humanity was the expression of that which was divine by the Holy Spirit, in love, in power, and specially in holiness. He was the Holy One of God. By the Holy Spirit He offered Himself without spot to God.

In all things He served His Father; but His service was the perfect presentation of

---

[16] Quite obviously, as well understood by the writer, "sin apart" (Hebrews 4:15).

what was divine, of the Father Himself, in
the midst of men—He, as to His humanity,
by the Spirit, at every moment answering
to the Godhead, the expression and efful-
gence of it without spot or blemish. All the
offerings of the Old Testament are types of
Christ; but in this connection the meat-of-
fering is the corresponding and most striking type. Cakes of fine flour, unleavened,
mingled with oil, anointed with oil, parted
in pieces, and oil poured upon them. What
a striking type of the humanity of Christ,
which, as to its nature, was of the Spirit,
and anointed with the Spirit, every part being characterised by the outpoured Spirit,
and by which all the incense of His perfec-
tions was offered up to God as a sweet-
smelling savour! So, He had to be tried by
fire, in death, to shew that all was a sweet
savour, and nothing else.

Finally, the power of the Holy Spirit was
shewn in the greatest and most perfect way
in the Lord's resurrection. Being put to
death in the flesh, He was quickened by the
Spirit. The Spirit, who in divine power
had been energetic in His birth, and in His
whole life, and by whom He at length offered Himself to God, manifested all His
power in quickening Jesus from death. It
is true indeed that He was raised from the
dead by the glory of the Father; also that
He Himself raised up His body, the temple
of God (John 2:19); but the Holy Spirit was

the immediate agent in His resurrection (1
Peter 3:18); the body also of the risen One
is a *spiritual* body.[17]

We repeat the question of some paragraphs ago: How important is the place of the Holy Spirit for the believer? The
answer, as we are seeing in Scripture is *all-important!* It
might be said, `Any and every Christian knows that' (true
enough); but, the practical difficulty is in fealty to—obedience
to—affection for—this same Holy Spirit. The apostle James
writes in the first chapter of his epistle, "But be ye doers of
[the] word and not hearers only, beguiling yourselves. For if
any man be a hearer of [the] word and not a doer, he is like to
a man considering his natural face in a mirror: for he has considered himself and is gone away, and straightway he has for-
gotten what he was like."

Is this not like ourselves? We can acknowledge scriptural
truths—give the nod to them—and then, perhaps, casually implement (or, worse—ignore) them in a practical way. The
prophet Jeremiah said, "Thy words were found, and I did eat
them, and thy words were unto me the joy and rejoicing of my
heart." That is the end result of fully appropriating Divine
truths—joy. The Lord spoke as to the good and faithful bondman in Matthew 25, "enter thou into the *joy* of thy lord." Do
we not wish the approval of the Lord, and to enter into *His*
joy? There is no joy like that.

---

[17] Extract: The Collected Writings of JN Darby, vol. 33, pgs. 314-316

We must notice, too, as a lateral consideration, that those addressed in this chapter of Matthew 25 are addressed as "bondman". Do any Christians think that they are exempt from having been discipled to the Lord—whatever other blessings are shown in scripture to be the believer's place—as a bondman? What more does the Lord say as to this? He says—and, very direct language it is—in Luke 17, "But which of you [is there] who, having a bondman ploughing or shepherding, when he comes in out of the field, will say, Come and lie down immediately to table? But will he not say to him, Prepare what I shall sup on, and gird thyself and serve me that I may eat and drink; and after that thou shalt eat and drink? Is he thankful to the bondman because he has done what was ordered? I judge not. Thus ye also, when ye shall have done all things that have been ordered you, say, We are unprofitable bondmen; we have done what it was our duty to do."

Why does the Lord phrase His words this way? He is certainly impressing us as to two things: (1) we have a service to provide as Christians—it is not optional—we are bondmen and (2) as it is our manifest duty to serve the great Servant Himself—it should be a joy to us and thus we would be delivered from self-exaltation by our service—it is required. Hebrews 12:28 clearly states, "let us serve God acceptably with reverence and fear." It is my sober judgment that many, if not most of us, take up our place before Christ somewhat casually. What does God say as to that? "Cursed be he that doeth the work of Jehovah negligently" (Jeremiah 48:10).

We have shown that the Bible characterizes the place of the Holy Spirit as all-important and that without the indwelling presence of the Holy Spirit we are "not of him" (see Romans 8:9)—that is to say, not of God. We have read in Romans 8:2 that the Holy Spirit is the "Spirit of life." We do not have our

54

natural life without the spirit given of God (Ecclesiastes 12:7)[18] and we most obviously cannot have a proper and eternal relationship with God unless, as just seen in Romans 8:2, we have it through the indwelling presence and power of the Holy Spirit. The Lord breathed the breath of life into Adam in Genesis 2 and in respect of His disciples in John 20:22 "he breathed into them, and says to them, Receive the Holy Spirit." The Holy Spirit, as seen already, is with us "forever"; thus, we are shown that we are now brought into eternal life.

Accordingly, when the Lord speaks to Nicodemus in John 3 about being born anew/again, He says that the Holy Spirit provides the capacitating power necessary to the believer's entrance into the kingdom of God. The Lord then almost immediately brings in the fact that the Cross (verse 14) provides the groundwork for the believer being brought into eternal life. This teaching on eternal life is subsequently reinforced in John 11:26 by the statement that the believer in Christ "shall never die." The point now being emphasized, though, is that it is through the indwelling power of the Holy Spirit that we are actually brought into eternal life (through faith, as said, in the Cross of Christ). Without His presence we simply do not have eternal life. The Lord is "the true God and eternal life" (1 John 5:20)—everything is centered in Him; however, it is only through His Spirit ("the Lord is the Spirit"—2 Corinthians 3:17) that we are brought into eternal life conditions. Romans 6:11 says, "reckon yourselves dead to sin and *alive to God in Christ Jesus*" (this is how we look at the way we are brought in); however, the actual power for this life is seen 1 Peter 3:18—"*made alive in the Spirit*." Thus, we understand what

---

[18] Notice the distinction between "spirit" as enabling our natural life and "Spirit" (capitalized) as showing a Person of the Godhead.

Paul writes in 1 Corinthians 15 (a quotation from Isaiah 25:8) "For this corruptible must needs put on incorruptibility, and this mortal put on immortality. But when this corruptible shall have put on incorruptibility, and this mortal shall have put on immortality, then shall come to pass the word written: Death has been swallowed up in victory. Where, O death, [is] thy sting? where, O death, thy victory?"

Without desiring to digress unduly, another point should be emphasized in passing (excuse the pun) and it is this: How can a Christian be shown as dying—and, yet, be said to "never die"? The answer is, again, to understand the practical in relation to the abstract. When the believer dies, the body—speaking typically—is put into a grave[19]. The person is, in this respect, dead—the apostle Paul writes in 1 Thessalonians 4 that, when the Lord comes for the Christian Church "*the dead in Christ* shall rise first" and "then we, the living who remain, shall be caught up together with them in [the] clouds, to meet the Lord in [the] air; and thus we shall be always with [the] Lord." Yet, just prior to this Paul writes, referring to the dead in Christ, as to those "who have fallen asleep through Jesus" —another aspect of this truth as to `never dying'. The thief on his cross said to the Lord who was next to him, "Remember me, [Lord,] when thou comest in thy kingdom. And Jesus said to him, Verily I say to thee, To-day shalt thou be with me in paradise" (Luke 23:42-43). In what condition was the thief when he went to Paradise? Was he dead? He did die; but, he was "asleep through Jesus" and with Him in Paradise. Both aspects of the truth can be seen—the body clearly would go

---

[19] i.e., a grave in the ground. The grave might be in the sea or somewhere else, including virtual annihilation through an explosion, etc.

into the grave, etc.; however, the "person" goes to be with the Lord.

This raises a lateral point which appears to be greatly misunderstood—even by intelligent, ministering Christians—and, it is this: using the thief as an immediate example, he was not and is not in some state, so to speak, of advanced awareness in Heaven. He is not in conversation with the Lord. He is not looking down on us here. He is not clambering around Heaven. He is asleep! The Holy Spirit's language in 1 Thessalonians 4 could not be any clearer—the Lord "with an assembling shout, with archangel's voice and with trump of God, shall descend from heaven; *and the dead in Christ shall rise first*; then we, the living who remain, shall be caught up together with them in [the] clouds, to meet the Lord in [the] air; and thus we shall be always with [the] Lord." If the "dead in Christ" had already risen and were active in some way in Heaven, there could be no "rising" of those who have gone before but are now asleep. It is a great thing to allow the truth of the Bible to form our thoughts rather than to attempt to interject natural notions into Scripture and muddle its truths.

Be Ye Holy for I am Holy

We now come to what is one of the most important points in this entire book: if every single Christian in the history of the Church from the day of Pentecost down to the present were properly and fully amenable to the lead of the Holy Spirit there would be NO divergence on Divine truths, no denominations—no divisions—no variations at all. In Joshua 18 we see that the divisions of the land for the children of Israel were entirely uneven and at least in part driven by the geography. In Ezekiel 47 and 48 the divisions are totally straight and parallel. This is like ourselves—speaking allegorically, we create what is uneven here according to the geography of our lives and circumstances; but, when we come to the Divine thought everything is straightly divided. If the natural mind was entirely set aside and only the lead of the Holy Spirit—the "unction" spoken of in 1 John 2:27—were followed, Christianity would truly and fully reflect Christ and would truly be the light of this world. These are simple, understandable realities—and, we have already quoted any number of scriptures showing that God is setting these realities before us. Scriptural examples include that Christians are to be "of one mind" (2 Corinthians 13:11; 1 Corinthians 1:10), and "Whoever has been begotten of God does not practise sin, because his seed abides in him, and he cannot sin, because he has been begotten of God" (1 John 3:9), and "Walk in [the] Spirit, and ye shall no way fulfil flesh's lust" (Galatians 5:16). There are a multitude of similar scriptures showing that, from the Divine perspective, Christianity is a perfect system engendered through the Cross of Christ and made practical and powerful through the indwelling Holy Spirit.

What I seek most to impress upon us is that the Bible clearly shows that God provides the capacitating power through the Holy Spirit and the available Divine resources (the "panoply" of Ephesians 6) to enable us to walk as overcomers here in an inimical scene. Jude records, "But to him that is able to keep you *without stumbling*, and to set [you] with exultation blameless before his glory, to the only God our Saviour, through Jesus Christ our Lord, [be] glory, majesty, might, and authority, from before the whole age, and now, and to all the ages. Amen." There is no occasion of stumbling in Heaven— this eulogy to God shows His power to keep us without stumbling *now* in this world. It is vital to get a hold of this point.

The fact of the matter is, as any honest Christian would agree, that it is the failure from OUR side that has caused the divisions, the variations, and the confusion as to doctrine in Christianity today. It needs to be stated that God is not unaware, reverently speaking, to the reality that we are going to sin. We do sin—we have alluded to this already in this book. However, that in itself cannot be an excuse. Paul queries in Romans 6, "What then shall we say? Should we continue in sin that grace may abound? Far be the thought. We who have died to sin, how shall we still live in it?" As presented in the Bible we are shown that we have a new nature that cannot sin (1 John 3:9), and, if we walk—as we are called to walk—in the "newness of life" (Romans 6:4) we are walking in the power of a nature that **cannot**, *in and of itself*, sin.

Both sides of the sin question are real and true. It is true that we have a new nature that is sinless—God's word sets this out. It is also true that we do sin. These two scriptures might appear to conflict in a nonsensical way; but, we are simply looking at two aspects of the truth—both very real. For example, Proverbs 26:4 states, "Answer not a fool according to his folly, lest thou also be like unto him." Proverbs 26:5 shows, "Answer a fool according to his folly, lest he be wise in his own eyes." Is the scripture confounded? Not at all—2 Timothy 3:16 says that, "Every scripture is divinely inspired", 1 Corinthians 14:33 states that, "God is not [a God] of disorder", and John 10:35 shows that, "the scripture cannot be broken." There cannot be any doctrinal conflict in what God sets out in the Bible and we have to understand how we are to work out the truth. The labor in this book is to set out that on this particular point as to sin there is a marked difference between dragging along in our Christian path here tied to and afflicted by a sinful nature; instead of, conversely, understanding that we are able to walk—always deferring to the lead of the Holy Spirit—in the power of a nature that in itself is without sin.

We must see what might appear to be only a subtle difference in practice between *trying* to be an upright Christian in distinction to *maintaining* the victory of the Cross. If we walk in the Spirit, we in NO WAY fulfill flesh's lust (already quoted earlier from Galatians 5:16). The Bible draws an immutable line between the old man and the new, between the natural mind and the spiritual (see, for example, 1 Corinthians 2:14—" But [the] natural man does not receive the things of the Spirit of God, for they are folly to him; and he cannot know [them] because they are spiritually discerned"), between the flesh and the Spirit—this reality cannot be emphasized enough. Again, I pause to emphasize—so that none of this appears to be mystical and unreal—that we all do sin; however, the Bible shows in Ephesians 4:24 that the new man "according to God is created in truthful righteousness and holiness" and we are to "put on" this man and "put off" the "old man". Holiness is a state without sin. 1 Peter 1 says distinctly, "but as he who has called you is holy, be ye also holy in all [your] conversation; because it is written, *Be ye holy, for I am holy*"—it hardly needs to be stated that, if we are called to be holy as God is holy, no sin is possible in this state.

This leads to the fact that Christianity, as has been mentioned, is a system created by God that is, in its inherent design, ordered and perfect. We must understand this. God has not just provided the Cross and the Holy Spirit, speaking reverently, and left it to us to work it out as we see fit. Not at all—the NT is full of teaching and admonition to the end that "These things I write to thee .... in order that *thou mayest know how one ought to conduct oneself in God's house*, which is [the] assembly of [the] living God, [the] pillar and base of the truth." In the type—in the tabernacle system under Moses— the pattern and procedures given for everything were exceedingly detailed and comprehensive and the exhortation as to this detail when it was given to Moses was repeated twice in Exodus 25. Towards the beginning of the chapter it was said, "And they shall make me a sanctuary, that I may dwell among them. *According to all that I shall shew thee*, the pattern of the tabernacle, and the pattern of all the utensils thereof, *even so shall ye make [it]*." Then, this same exhortation was further emphasized by the Lord at the end of the chapter by Him saying, "And <u>see</u> that <u>thou</u> make [them] according to their pattern, which hath been shewn to thee in the mountain."

It is inconceivable that God, in accord with His nature, would create anything that, in its pristine state, could be imperfect. We can go back to the biblical statements as to simple creation in Genesis 1—"And God saw everything that he had made, and behold it was very good." Notice, again, the "*very good.*" It might be argued that some people are born deformed or with certain impairments; however, that is a result of the fall of man in the Garden of Eden. In pristine creation the Holy

61

Spirit's record stands (inclusive of man)—"very good"—and of man—the highest level of creation—it is actually said, "And God created Man *in his image*, in the image of God created he him; male and female created he them." We cannot consider that there might be any imperfections in what is created in the image of God Himself in unsullied creation.

If we look at all this, so to speak, from the reverse it can further help in its understanding. Did God create a flawed creation?[20] The language of Scripture as just quoted above shows not. Has God created Christianity to be imperfect, so that there would be divisions and contrary doctrines? Absolutely not— the Church is spoken of as being "a habitation of God in the Spirit" (Ephesians 2:22). Would God, thus, have in mind to create a flawed habitation for Himself? We see in Revelation 21 that the Church—looked at in those verses as the Bride, the Lamb's wife—is also looked at as "the *holy* city, Jerusalem, coming down out of the heaven from God, *having the glory of God.* Her shining [was] like a most precious stone, as a crystal-like jasper stone". There are no flaws—it is like a *most precious* stone. Of course, the Church in its practical display shows a multitude of flaws today; however, that is from

---

[20] Genesis 1:2 says that "the earth was waste and empty, and darkness was on the face of the deep"; but, as has been said by others, something came into creation initially to cause this since Isaiah 45:18 shows that "not as waste did he create it: he formed it to be inhabited."

It might also be argued that God created Man at least somewhat flawed since Adam and Eve ate of the forbidden fruit in the Garden of Eden; however, this is begging the question since Ecclesiastes 7 says, "God made man upright." In a like argument, it could be suggested that Satan (and, by extension, some of the other angels) were created flawed since Satan fell; however, again, we see in Isaiah 14 that God created Lucifer with preeminence—the language is that he was "son of the morning".

failures on our side and the great need is to see the Church both in its inherent nature and in ultimate result as God has set it out in Scripture.

There are at a foundational level, in a sense, only two perspectives as to how Christians are going to work out Christianity today in the early 21st century. One is based on the Bible; the other is colored by naturally-minded reasons.

The first could be stated, perhaps, as: Christianity is clearly a Divine realm designed by God that brings the redeemed soul into an intimate, eternal relationship with God through the power of the Holy Spirit—and it involves a new creation for man ("So if any one [be] in Christ, [there is] a new creation"— 2 Corinthians 5:17). I see that, in this new creation, as such, there is no sin—and that my attitude is to be that of an over-comer walking "in the Spirit". When I do sin (because I fail to be governed by the lead of the Holy Spirit; but, instead, accede to the influences of the mind of the flesh) my immediate re-course is " If we confess our sins, he is faithful and righteous to forgive us [our] sins, and cleanse us from all unrighteous-ness" – 1 John 1:9. In this way the harmonious character of my relationship with Divine Persons is then restored.[21] The inviolate principles of Scripture are to govern our Christian path here even in a day of breakdown, and, as Christians are called upon to cling to the truth ("Buy the truth, and sell it not"—Proverbs 23:23) I am going to do *that* come what may.

---

[21] Of course, "what a man sows he shall reap" reminds us that, while the penalty for sin being death is removed for faith in the Cross of Christ, the *actions* of sin can linger. If I assault my neighbor and then confess such a grievous action to the Lord, His blood has cleansed from all sin (1 John 1:7) but I might yet be led away to jail. In this respect see 2 Samuel 12 and Psalm 51:4

I see that the first and great commandment is "Thou shalt love [the] Lord thy God with all thy heart, and with all thy soul, and with all thy understanding" and I am in total focus on that. The Lord said in John 14:15, "*If* ye love me, keep my commandments" and I see that the proof of my love is regarded by Him as keeping His commandments—all of his commandments—not just the ones that suit me. The apostle John writes, "He that says, I know him, and does not keep his commandments, is a liar, and the truth is not in him; but whoever keeps his word, *in him verily the love of God is perfected. Hereby we know that we are in him.*"

I continue by seeing that the second commandment is like the first—"Thou shalt love thy neighbour as thyself"; but, I see that the first commandment has preeminence and that is why it is characterized as the *first and great* commandment. If I love God in the way that the Scripture expresses that I should love Him, the second commandment will, reflexively, be properly fulfilled—"He that loves his brother abides in light, and there is no occasion of stumbling in him" (1 John 2). But, I cannot reverse the order and put my brother before my responsibilities to God Himself. If my brother is an unrepentant fornicator I cannot allow my love for him to gloss over the sin to the result that God's interests and commandments are put into second place.

The above constitutes, in a general way, the first of these two Christian perspectives.

The other perspective might, as a general statement in respect of many Christian fellowships briefly be summed up as: We know that there are many divisions and denominations in Christendom today, and that many Christians cannot seem to agree on various points of doctrine. However, we'll do the best we can. None of us is perfect—we're all sinners here. It's good to not make waves — and as we really cannot substantially change the inconsistencies we must just continue along in spite of the differences that exist. Even though there are concerns as to different practices and doctrine—as long as there is no glaring evil—we will go along together (after all, we're all Christians). We should not judge one another—we can all worship God in our own way and it is only being brotherly and loving to be able to agree to disagree.

This second perspective is, as we have been laboring to accentuate, contrary to Scripture. It inherently accepts the presence of disunity—perhaps largely because the disunity simply appears to be the "status quo". Even on the simplest level, however, full unity is the Divine expectation—"Shall two walk together except they be agreed?" (Amos 3:3). This is not to say that problems and issues do not arise in a fellowship—Satan is very busy and every Christian is engaged in an active, spiritual warfare (Ephesians 6:12). However, Christians are called upon to meet what is wrong as it arises (1 Corinthians 5:12-13; Matthew 18:15-18). This involves striving to keep unity—something we have already quoted (Ephesians 4:3)—and it is important to recognize that the Bible defines proper unity as "the unity of the Spirit". In this respect, "God is one" (Galatians 3:20)—there is no disagreement, reverently speaking, in the Godhead; thus, any unity that is of the Holy Spirit will be in accord with all the Persons of the Godhead and must be, reflexively, in accord with Divine principles and precepts. Any allowed disunity cannot be sanctioned by the Lord—Paul writes in 2 Timothy 2:13, "if we are unfaithful, he abides faithful, for he cannot deny himself." It is recorded in 2 Chronicles 15:2, "Jehovah is with you while ye are with him"—i.e., in this scripture *His* relationship with us is first based upon our fidelity in *our* relationship with Him. God, of course, has initially approached us unilaterally on the basis of "being rich in mercy, because of his great love wherewith he loved us" (Ephesians 2:14). However, when it comes to *our* maintenance of the truth that God has provided to us we have, as scripture shows, every ability and, reflexively, every responsibility to fulfill righteousness. Jude writes, "Beloved, using all diligence to write to you of our common salvation, I have been obliged to write to you *exhorting [you] to contend earnestly for the faith* once delivered to the saints."

We can quote again in John 4:24 "*God [is] a spirit*; and they who worship him must worship [him] in spirit and truth." We must notice that John records that God [is] a *spirit*. Of course, one Person of the Godhead has entered into manhood to bring believers home to God; however, this in no way changes that God *is spirit*, and *must be* worshipped *in spirit* and truth. Nothing could be plainer than this statement. It might be asked; but, we are clearly in flesh here—how does this integrate? Again, although still in earthly circumstances, we must yet weigh the moral thrust of scriptural teaching. So, the tenor of the teaching in the Bible—"flesh and blood cannot inherit the kingdom of God"—goes well beyond the physical to include the moral/spiritual—"ye are not in flesh but in Spirit, if indeed God's Spirit dwell in you" (Romans 8:9). To help us understand this aspect of scriptural doctrine we then also have in 2 Corinthians 4:7, as quoted earlier in this book, "But we have this treasure in earthen vessels"—God recognizes our earthly condition. However, the apostle highlights that the existence of the earthen vessel is not to excuse unrighteousness as he then concludes—we quote this scripture again—"that the surpassingness of the power may be of God, and not from us." We have the Divinely given power to fulfill righteousness.

Love—the Power for Righteousness

We have now come to what might be stated to be at the core of our Christian calling—love. Love provides the catalyzing power in any relationship—how much more so in our Christian relations with God and man. We need, at this juncture, to take a step back as we consider what is likely the most liberating of all truths in Scripture, and how we are to work out our Christian calling in respect of this truth.

We have been considering doctrine—and, doctrine is vital—it has been likened to the banks of a river. Doctrine helps keep the Christian from meandering outside of the prescribed course of the river. However, Christianity involves, as stated earlier in this book, a relationship with Divine Persons, other Christians and men in general. The character of these relationships in Christianity ultimately go—as with any relationship—substantially beyond what we might carefully refer to as the simple do's and don'ts of the relationship.

We certainly cannot dispense with scriptural doctrine while here on this earth—as to this the Lord spoke in particular in Matthew 5:18: "For verily I say unto you, Until the heaven and the earth pass away, one iota or one tittle shall in no wise pass from the law till all come to pass." Certainly, the moral *principles* of doctrinal teachings in the Bible are timeless, as well. But, as certainly, we won't need nor will there be present the Bible in Heaven—"knowledge, it shall be done away"—1 Corinthians 13:8. There shall be no further spiritual growth—all will be in moral perfection and each Christian with a body of glory (see 1 Corinthians 15:40-49). John further writes in his first epistle—"Beloved, now are we children of God, and what we shall be has not yet been manifested; we know that if it is manifested we shall be like him" (1 John 3:2).

Speaking of Heaven, what is to be the character of our eternity as provided by our God of love? We shall be in the presence of the Father, in the company of the Lord and capacitated for that eternal setting through the everlasting, indwelling presence of the Holy Spirit. It will be an eternity in which—in the mutuality of unhindered love—we will enjoy, and will provide enjoyment to, the infinite God of love with whom we even now have to do in so many wonderful ways. If we look at natural creation with its almost limitless detail and beauties, we can readily recognize that Heaven surely will in an ascendant way showcase, speaking reverently, the nature of our God of love in immeasurable detail and glory. Indeed, the Bible speaks specifically to this in saying, "Things which eye has not seen, and ear not heard, and which have not come into man's heart, which God has prepared for them that love him" (1 Corinthians 2:9). We see the descriptions—largely allegorical—in The Revelation chapter 21 as to the heavenly realm which is our home—the language suggests to us (to be taken up in a spiritual way, of course) what God has prepared. In this respect we must note that "the glory of God has enlightened it"—all will be eternally to the glory of God and the presentation in Revelation 21 is set out in the scriptures as the pinnacle of the display of that glory.

Turning back to our earthly Christian testimony we are reminded afresh that even though we are on earth our heavenly calling is to define the pattern for our earthly walk—"have your mind on the things [that are] above, not on the things [that are] on the earth"—Colossians 3:2. We must now consider again an already-quoted truth that every Christian knows—and it is this: "God is love." Thus, referring back to this issue of "relationship", here is a question: `If God is love, what should be our proper response to Him?' Wouldn't a proper response to a God of love involve *our* full love? Would this mean all our love without any hindrance; or, would most or part of our love suffice? The reality is that if we are at all lackluster in our love—we are then denying God the fullness of the relationship that He has in mind. Why is the first commandment phrased this way—"Love the Lord thy God *with all thy heart*" (Matthew 27:37)?

Here, then, is the great test that we have been gradually approaching in the prior pages of this book. Here is the simple question for each and every one of us: Do you love the Lord *with all your heart*? Are you, in a constitutional way, unrestrained in your love and affection for Him? Are His interests always first; or, will you modify His interests—*and, therefore, scriptural precepts*—so that your own, natural interests edge into preeminence? Do you engage in anything —even momentarily (or, in a more concerted way, by actively pursuing some course in this life)—that you recognize, both from scripture and also from the guilty feeling you have as a result of the unction from the Holy Spirit, is not pleasing to the Lord? Why would we do anything that is unpleasing to the Lord? After all, He loved us with such a love that He endured the Cross so that we can not only be reconciled to God but spend eternity in Paradise with Him. Paul writes, "the Son of God, who has loved *me* and given himself for me" (Galatians 2:20)—does this not apply to each of us? Forget for the moment, if you will, the next fellow—you (each of us) have an individual relationship with the Lord—is it a strong, healthy and full relationship; or, is it in any way lackluster?

If you—if all of us as Christians—are willing to admit that we, even if only at intervals, are governed by our own natural desires to the end that we set aside the Lord's commandments, then we are now coming to what we might refer to as the crux of the reason why—even as Christians—we sin and why, by extension, there is so much error, confusion and division in Christendom.

We've already seen that the Lord says distinctly, "If ye love me, keep my commandments" (John 14:15), and it has been mentioned that this is phrased in this way to highlight that the proof of our love is in keeping His commandments. Fidelity is, properly, tied to love. If I tell my wife that I love her and then leave the house to carouse with partygoers and possibly to dally with some other woman—it is possible that in a flawed way I might love her; but, irrespective of that, there is *no immediate proof* of love *nor, if I do have love for her, is the love for my wife in any way a full and proper love.* A poor analogy, perhaps; but, I trust that this crude depiction emphasizes the point at hand—and possibly more so in view of the fact that as Christians we form the Bride of Christ.

1 Corinthians 13 presents in the most substantive way the nature of love in respect of the testimonial path of the Christian here in this world. The apostle writes that if I "have not love, *I am nothing*" and "if I deliver up my body that I may be burned, but have not love, *I profit nothing.*" The secret to this section is to recognize that the catalyst for all that the Christian should be and do is .... Love. This must be so since "God is love" and we are His sons—having "become partakers of the divine nature" (2 Peter 1:4). The last verse of this chapter in 1 Corinthians 13 reinforces this matter of love by stating, "and now abide faith, hope, love; these three things; *and the greater of these [is] love.*" From where is this love to be derived? From and through Christ. Even natural love in this world is a result of man being made by the Lord in the image

of God. The natural love, of course, is corrupted through the moral fall of man; but, in 1 John the apostle is explicit in his explanations as to love—particularly Christian love—and in chapter 4 he writes, "Beloved, if God has so loved us, we also ought to love one another. No one has seen God at any time: if we love one another, *God abides in us, and his love is perfected in us.*"

When the Lord commences addressing the seven assemblies in the beginning chapters of the book of The Revelation we have as a preface, "These things says he that holds the seven stars in his right hand, who walks in the midst of the seven golden lamps" (Revelation 2:1). These are the lamps, or, lights, of the testimony of the seven assemblies (the assemblies being representative of the entire Church) that we have already discussed earlier. The Lord then begins in chapter 2 with Ephesus—the assembly that had received the highest doctrinal teaching in the epistles of Paul (who was himself the "wise architect"—1 Corinthians 3:10—of the Church). The Lord's estimation, as always, takes into consideration both what is right and what is wrong. The Lord says in accreditation, "I know thy works and [thy] labour, and thine endurance, and that thou canst not bear evil [men]; and thou hast tried them who say that themselves [are] apostles and are not, and hast found them liars; and endurest, and hast borne for my name's sake, and hast not wearied".

If you were part of Ephesus at that time, might you feel assured—with the Lord's language as shown above—that all is well? Do we not do this in our Christian path here—i.e., approve ourselves based on what is right; but, perhaps, sidestep what is wrong? We need to have full and proper assessments that bear the scrutiny of reality. The issues in Christendom today are not about what is right; *but, about what is wrong.*

The Lord's very next statement—after His approbation of all that is right with Ephesus—is this, "I have <u>against</u> thee, *that thou hast left thy first love.* Remember therefore whence thou art fallen, and repent, and do the first works: but if not, I am coming to thee, and I will remove thy lamp out of its place, except thou shalt repent."

This language is striking and should be sobering to every honest Christian. First, the Lord is saying that He has something "against thee." I can say, as an aside, that I do not want, myself, to be in a position where the Lord is considering my circumstances and saying that He has something *against* me! In what He says here we must notice that the Lord is not saying that there was *no* love for Him. He is not even suggesting here that the love was entirely lackluster. What He is saying is that "the first love"—which we can take to be that full response of love—had been relinquished. Their love for Him had suffered a reduction. Accordingly, He defines the need for repentence—He repeats it twice which shows the emphasis placed upon it.

What do we learn from this? Is it not accurate to say—according as it is shown in this section of The Revelation—that, if we as Christians are not in full and first response in love to the Lord's great love, He is displeased and has something against us? That is what it says, isn't that so? Is He not placing a critical emphasis upon the depth and nature of our love for Himself? As a result of the reduction of love He applies the same word that is used in respect of sin—"repent".[22] Could

[22] While we are emphasizing "love" it does us well to be reminded of another aspect of the truth—"The fear of Jehovah is the beginning of wisdom" (Proverbs 9:10). We cannot willfully trifle with God—"And to every one to whom much has been given, much shall be required from him"

any say, after reading and considering His words in this section, that the intensity of our love doesn't matter much to Him? That, as long as we have any degree of response in love towards Him He is well pleased? No—He is gauging our love and defining it accordingly—He is that God with a plumb line in His hand (see Amos 7). Read Malachi 1 to see with Israel the Lord's estimation when His people are casual or uncaring in their response to Him.

(Luke 12:48). Hebrews 10:26-27 states, "For where we sin wilfully after receiving the knowledge of the truth, there no longer remains any sacrifice for sins, but a certain fearful expectation of judgment, and heat of fire about to devour the adversaries."

Sons of God

We have now come to the heart of this book. What we have been seeing, is that Christianity is, at its simplest level, a love matter. This has to be true, as God is love. We have touched upon the fact that any relationship He is seeking would, of necessity and in proper keeping with His nature, involve the full character of love. We have already queried, `Would a God of love desire a half-hearted response from the creature whom He has called into relationship with Himself?' We are Sons of God and are expected to be in proper response to that calling!

Thus, the internal promptings—if we can refer to them in this way—that lead us as Christians in our path here through life come from either of two natures. One nature is of God and the promptings are from the Holy Spirit—"And when ye turn to the right hand or when ye turn to the left, thine ears shall hear a word behind thee, saying, This is the way, walk ye in it" (Isaiah 30:21)—as we have already quoted . The fruits of this nature are seen in Galatians 5—"But the fruit of the Spirit is love, joy, peace, long-suffering, kindness, goodness, fidelity, meekness, self-control: against such things there is no law. But they that [are] of the Christ have crucified the flesh with the passions and the lusts. If we live by the Spirit, let us walk also by the Spirit."

The other nature is the old man—the sinful nature—and its promptings are always related to "self" and inherently reject the authority of God. This is fully set out in Romans 7. This is the nature that is accessible to Satan, and the fruits of this nature are also set out in Galatians 5—"Now the works of the flesh are manifest, which are fornication, uncleanness,

74

licentiousness, idolatry, sorcery, hatred, strifes, jealousies, angers, contentions, disputes, schools of opinion, envyings, murders, drunkennesses, revels, and things like these; as to which I tell you beforehand, even as I also have said before, that they who do such things shall not inherit God's kingdom."

On the simplest level, therefore, our path here morally as Christians is governed by choices we constantly make throughout each day. We are led to make these choices and judgments either by the morally right lead of the Holy Spirit or by the old man "which corrupts itself according to the deceitful lusts" (Ephesians 4:22). If we only ever made choices and judgments by—if we were entirely regulated by—were fully amenable to—the lead of the Holy Spirit ..... would we make sinful choices? The obvious answer is "No". We've already highlighted this fact. As we've quoted earlier in Galatians 5, "Walk in [the] Spirit, and ye shall *in no way* fulfil flesh's lust."

The Holy Spirit would NEVER lead us into sin—"Let no man, being tempted, say, I am tempted of God. For God cannot be tempted by evil things, and himself tempts no one. But every one is tempted, drawn away, and enticed by his own lust" (James 1:13). The entire message of this book you are now reading is aimed at several scriptural truths and we reiterate one of them as this:

the Holy Spirit provides the capacitating power so that we can fulfill righteousness here on this earth.

The apostle Paul writes in 2 Corinthians 13:7, "that ye may do what is right." This should not be burdensome—Christianity involves liberty before God (within, of course, the parameters of what is scriptural)—"be ye not as a horse, as a mule, which have no understanding: whose trappings must be bit and bridle, for restraint, or they will not come unto thee" (Psalm 32:9). The Lord said, "the truth shall set you free" (John 8:32). Free from what? Free from everything and anything that, in an ultimate result, hinders our relationship in righteousness with a holy God. We have been "set free from the bondage of corruption into the *liberty* of the glory of the children of God" (Romans 8:21). The yoke from the Lord is easy and any burden from himself is light (see Matthew 11:30)—wonderful grace!

Thus, this great and infinitely liberating truth in Christianity is—to emphasize again—that we are to be confirmed in our minds that it is in the power of the Holy Spirit (and only through His indwelling power) that we can live, move and properly function in the spiritual realm into which we've been brought through God's calling and the wonderful results of the Cross of Christ. This may appear somewhat self-evident (and, it should). It is also evident that preachers throughout Christendom exhort in weekly sermons that Christianity involves practical, experimental implementation of scriptural truths; yet, clear teaching as to the *power* and the moral state by which this is accomplished is so often left out of the preaching. This is partially because "deliverance", as spoken of earlier in this book, is not properly understood and therefore not communicated. The congregant is left understanding that righteousness should be in place; but, not necessarily understanding that the righteous nature is *already in place*, and the ability to *maintain* that righteousness is already in place—resident—in the Holy Spirit. As alluded to much earlier in this book, it is not a question of *attaining* righteousness; but, rather, *maintaining* the righteous estate we are given through new birth and the power of the Holy Spirit. Huge difference.

Inherent in this reality is that to exercise this liberating power we must "not *grieve* the Holy Spirit of God with which ye have been sealed" (Ephesians 4:30). We can surely be agreed as Christians that, if we demur as to the voice and lead of the Holy Spirit and instead favor our natural will, we have immediately grieved the Holy Spirit. If a father instructs his son in some moral issue—and the son refuses the admonition—is not the father grieved over this matter? Of course the father is grieved—his son is refusing to make right judgment.

The Book of Revelation is largely a book showing judgments. In the very first chapter the Lord—the Lover of His Church—is, yet, seen "girt about at the breasts with a golden girdle" (restraint, for the moment, of the heart's affections in lieu of judgments), "his eyes as a flame of fire" (fire invariably represents judgment in scripture) and "out of his mouth a sharp two-edged sword going forth" (the word of God in judgment and power).

Let's further the example of the father and the son as noted above. Let us say that the son continues to refuse the father's right and additional admonitions—either as to the same issue or, perhaps, lateral or even diverse issues. The father is continually further grieved. The relationship is becoming more substantially affected. As the son is in denial as to aspects of what is right, he is, of necessity, drifting away from the truth. His practical path is now reflecting this moral departure (perhaps unseen to others; but, known to the father). If he continues on in his refusals he will, in reflex, likely be subsequently more open to and accepting of contingent error. Using the analogy above and considering the father as a type of God's authority implemented through the Holy Spirit, we can say that the son is losing his moral compass. We can see in the OT type of the "unmanageable and rebellious son" in

Deuteronomy 21 that God has an extremely sobering view of rebellion.

The further step to grieving the Holy Spirit—an infinitely more sobering step—is to *quench* the Holy Spirit. "Quench not the Spirit" (1 Thessalonians 5:19). In this step, the moral guidance system, speaking reverently, is disconnected. True Christians cannot lose the Holy Spirit, of course—cannot become unsaved, cannot become unborn-again; but, in the practical path here the voice of the Holy Spirit has been quenched. There can no longer be a proper representation of Christ in such Christians. The testimony is being harmed[23] since the outward position is that of Christians but the power has been lost in the inward side to walk properly as Christians.

The next and final step to this sad circumstance is that the matters and moral state of any might well be such that a state is introduced which entails "a sin unto death" (1 John 5:16) in which we are not even to pray for such. What a terrible state in which to be as a child of God; and, yet, I have known some number of true Christians like that—saved for eternity, certainly; but, who have "made shipwreck as to the faith."

I believe that, with many if not most Christians, the place of the Lord as Savior is seen, and the place of the Father as representing God ("to us there is one God, the Father"—1 Corinthians 8:6) is essentially recognized; but, the place of the Holy Spirit appears, perhaps, a bit vague. Yet, without His

---

[23] See, in this regard of damage to the testimony, 2 Samuel 12, "thou hast given great occasion to the enemies of Jehovah to blaspheme."

presence, power and lead we cannot experimentally[24] be sons of God ("for as many as are *led* by [the] Spirit of God, these are sons of God"—Romans 8:14). Without the Holy Spirit we could never enter into full, final and proper relationship with the Lord ("if any one has not [the] Spirit of Christ he is not of him"—Romans 8:9). Without the Holy Spirit's' guidance we cannot properly walk righteously here ("If we live by the Spirit, let us *walk also by* the Spirit"—Galatians 5:25), and without the indwelling presence of the Holy Spirit we cannot become the inheritors of eternal life (He is "the Spirit of life"—Romans 8:2).

A proper understanding as to all that we have been discussing—the definitive dividing line between the old man and the new man—enables the Cross of Christ to be better understood. The reverse, of course, is true—a clear understanding of the Cross helps us to see the complete removal, as we have been saying, of the old man. In and through that Cross God has removed the man offensive to His eye—the old man[25]—and provided the basis for man to be brought, through faith, into salvation and eternal life. With Israel we see that, as a general type, the unregenerate, unrepentant and unholy nations of the promised land (the earthly inheritance) into which Israel was brought were to be destroyed. Once destroyed, they could not affect Israel morally. This same principle is seen in the Cross.

---

[24] We are, of course, sons of God in title and inheritance; however, it is only as "led" by the Holy Spirit that we are practically (experimentally) in the gain of this.

[25] Christ, of course, the sin-bearer, was Himself without sin ("tempted in all things in like manner, sin apart"—Hebrews 4:15); however, on the Cross, "Him who knew not sin he has made sin for us" (2 Corinthians 5:21).

An old nature put to death cannot have an effect upon that which has been made alive in the power of the Holy Spirit. Thus, we can fully understand the admonition—putting "to death the deeds of the body" (Romans 8:13).

It is of note that the nations the Israelites could not dispossess were able to subsequently lead them astray. David provided garrisons during his rule to control such; but, in Israel's further history, those of the garrisoned nations were able to rebel. Is not this like us? We have some elements of our old nature that we have successfully put to death—other elements, though, perhaps, we have only been able to garrison (certainly, better than not being garrisoned); but, they can plague us again over time because we have not fully put to death those features of the flesh through the application of the Cross in our own lives.

The primary reason that characteristics of the flesh are not put to death must be that there is, ultimately, a certain lack of full committal to Christ. This, in turn, then undoubtedly leads to a certain soft judgment as to those particular features of the flesh. We can see this with Lot when he was led by the angels out of Sodom and Gomorrah—he was being delivered from a city that was marked for destruction; but he sought refuge in an adjacent city. First, he "lingered"—do we not tend to linger over decisively judging features of the flesh? Then, after being told to flee to the mountains he evidently still wanted the features offered by a city—his language was, "Behold now, this city is near to flee to, and it is small: I pray thee, let me escape thither—*is it not small?*—and my soul shall live". Our tendency is to discount as "small" what we want to retain—"Oh, it's nothing—it's not so bad—others do it", etc. The clear directive to him was to flee to the mountain—it's been noted that Abraham was on the mount with God (Hebron is in the

Judean mountains—an elevation of some 3,000 feet) inter-
ceding for Lot who had chosen to dwell in the plain which was
"thoroughly watered, like the land of Egypt." In our first/old
nature we will always choose what is represented in the land
of Egypt.

We have woven through the paragraphs of this book various
aspects of divine truths and precepts as set out in the Bible—
and we can now reemphasize two clarion truths in respect of
our Christian estate and in view of working out our path in
proper testimony here:

*(1) the all-important, all-vital place and power of the Holy
Spirit and (2) the place of love in its activity.*

We cannot separate these truths as any direction and lead
from the Holy Spirit is from a God who is, inherently, love. In
other words, we cannot say that the Holy Spirit would be leading us in proper fidelity to the truth; but that, somehow, love
forms no part of His leading.

If God is love, and it is love that prompted Him, reverently
speaking, to create Man in His image in view of an eternal relationship in love and affection, and if we have become sons
of Himself (a race of firstborn ones), and if we have "become
partakers of the Divine nature", and if we (through new birth)
have something introduced in us that is sinless, and if we have
become indwelt by God Himself in the power of the Holy
Spirit—while we certainly are not God, as His creatures we
cannot have been brought any closer to Himself than as shown
above. We must tread carefully here—we must stay within the
bounds of Scripture; yet, we can see the truth of all that has
just been related in the last few sentences. Astounding reality!
Only God could have conceived and then implemented such a

reality. In Man's primary history and lineage as seen in Luke 3 we see, as we trace in reverse the Lord's lineage, the grace and affection in the Holy Spirit's record—"of Noe, of Lamech, of Methusala, of Enoch, of Jared, of Maleleel, of Cainan, of Enos, of Seth, *of Adam, of God.*

What person could be born in sin and corruption, as David records in Psalm 51—"Behold, in iniquity was I brought forth, and in sin did my mother conceive me"—and then be born again to a sinless estate? From a natural perspective, "That which is crooked cannot be made straight" (Ecclesiastes 1:15). In response to the disciples astonishment as to "who can be saved" in Mark 10, the Lord's own words are, "With men it is impossible, but not with God; for all things are possible with God." What manifest goodness and grace of God towards all men as it says in Titus 2:11—"For the grace of God which carries with it salvation for all men has appeared"!

Think of one Man effectuating salvation for all men! Men here assign committees and regularly marshal considerable efforts in seeking to accomplish even average results—think of God appointing one Man only and being able to rest in His perfect accomplishments! The infirm man of John 5 said, in response to the Lord's query as to whether he wished to be well, "Sir, I have not a man, in order, when the water has been troubled, to cast me into the pool; but while I am coming another descends before me" (John 5:7). *I have not a man.* What does the Lord say to him? "Arise, take up thy couch and walk." No angel, no troubling of the water—only the Lord and His command in love and grace. *We* have a Man! What a Man we have in our glorious Savior!

So, here is what I wish to reiterate to you: if we obviate the will of the Holy Spirit in our lives (His lead in any matter or question) and, instead, follow the promptings of the old man in his sinful nature—are we not ultimately displaying a lack of affection and love towards the Lord? Are we not immediately guilty of displaying a lack of fidelity? Are we not substituting our natural interests instead of His interests? Are we not being unfaithful? There could not without argument be any other answer to the above four questions than "Yes". We cannot leave out Christian growth, of course; yet, ultimately, every true Christian—young or old—has the indwelling presence and unction from the Holy Spirit which always results in such being led into the truth—"the truth as is in Jesus" (Ephesians 4:21). We have to be careful not to mix up Christian growth with Christian spirituality. The boy Samuel was young; but, he was girded with a linen ephod (1 Samuel 2:18). As noted, the practical power in Christianity for us here is derived from love towards the Lord and faithfulness to the lead of the Holy Spirit who will always lead us into all that pertains to Christ.

You might say, "But, this is obvious." Yes—it is; but, the point here—and, this embraces an infinitely important comprehension—is that for the true Christian, as a general statement—and, especially, for the long-established Christian—allowed iniquity (whether small or large) must, of necessity, ultimately trace back to some lack of fidelity to the Lord. He is the Head to His Body (Colossians 1:18) and also the Head to every man (1 Corinthians 11:13)—He has this authority in Headship and if His Headship is ignored it is a contrary willfulness. Thus, speaking typically, either there is some abiding lack in whatever degree of genuine and deep affection for Himself; or, alternately, if the Christian is indeed constitutionally faithful, a decision at a particular moment was made to decidedly deny the voice of the Holy Spirit.

A perfect example of this latter circumstance is King David. He was not only the "anointed of Jehovah" (1 Samuel 10) but he was the "sweet psalmist of Israel" (2 Samuel 23:1). He was not only a strong warrior for the rights of the Lord (a great type of the Lord Himself as Savior) but was also able to play in such skill on the harp (a type of the instrumentality, reverently speaking, of the Holy Spirit) that he could displace an evil spirit. His Psalms speak to his piety and spiritual intelligence. Yet, he most obviously displaced and shut out any voice from the Holy Spirit in the matter of Bathsheba the wife of Urijah the Hittite—a grievous sin. "See that ye refuse not him that speaks"—Hebrews 12:25.

In respect of the above statements it is only equitable to notice that the OT does speak of "the sin of inadvertence" (Leviticus 4)—in this way the Holy Spirit is taking account of some sin as to which the sinner was unaware of the transgression. Thus, there is a certain difference (it is all regarded in the Bible as sin, of course) between somebody willfully sinning in respect of some issue and somebody who was unaware that some particular divine precept had been transgressed—and, we can bring this principle forward to our day. In a best case, we can link it to Christian growth (i.e., considering that some might be young, "uniformed" Christians—which would further highlight the need for distinctive, scriptural teaching in a fellowship—evidently an obvious problem today throughout Christendom); in a worst case, we can likely link it to indifference. I can recall being in a business meeting over twenty years ago and the meeting—attended by a good ratio of believing Christians—was started by a woman—instead of by a brother—standing up to pray. I later contacted the organizer—a Christian woman—and indicated to her that "I will that the *men* pray in every place" (1 Timothy 2:8). She was totally unaware of this scripture; but, immediately said to me that they would cease such a practice of women praying publicly instead of men—as to which I was glad to hear.

However, why should she—as an adult Christian having been many years a Christian—been unaware of such a basic NT scripture? As Christians we have been made the benefactors of a continual lead from the Holy Spirit, and from Him we also have an unction—"yourselves, the unction which ye have received from him abides in you, and ye have not need that any one should teach you; but as the same unction teaches you as to all things, and is true and is not a lie, and even as it has taught you, ye shall abide in him" (1 John 2:27). I have sometimes quoted an elemental scripture to a Christian friend only to get the query, "What is that scripture? and, where is it in the Bible?" It can only be a lack of interest that results in someone not taking up their Bible. Daily reading is best ("He wakeneth morning by morning, he wakeneth mine ear to hear as the instructed"—Isaiah 50:4) to study God's Word. Billy Graham evidently spoke to the effect that many Christians' Bibles sit largely unused on the top shelf. Would all this not show a result of a certain indifference to Christ and the Heavenly calling?

Another point in reference to our fidelity to Christ is that how each of us acts affects all other Christians and the Christian testimony. This is to say, that if we act poorly as Christians it casts a negative light on Christianity and therefore other Christians (not to speak of being dishonoring to the Lord). The story is told as to a Christian who went into immoral circumstances—another Christian said to him, "You took me with you." Conversely, if we act in fidelity to the Lord it not only provides a proper light for men (Matthew 5:15); but, is clearly an encouragement to other Christians ("For we have great thankfulness and encouragement through thy love, because the bowels of the saints are refreshed by thee, brother"—Philemon 6:7).

It is interesting in respect of what we may refer to as being the "corporate" side of Christianity that, in the Book of Esther, Mordecai refused to bow to Haman since he was a wicked man. Haman, as a result, sought to destroy not only Mordecai but all the Jews. This is the aim of Satan—his ultimate desire is to destroy all that pertains to God. We certainly do not want to give way to Satan. It is most important to recognize that, even in a day of public breakdown such as is existent in Christendom today, "the firm foundation of God stands, having this seal, [The] Lord knows those that are his; and, Let every one who names the name of [the] Lord withdraw from iniquity." (2 Timothy 2:19). Mordecai's circumstances were that of being in a day of breakdown in respect of Israel—Judah had been brought into captivity by Nebuchadnezzar King of Babylon according to God's edict—yet, Mordecai himself was faithful to God and the Lord wrought through him and Esther a great deliverance to His earthly people at that time. We are never called upon to relinquish faithfulness just because of broken Christian circumstances. There are many divisions and much error in Christendom today that show clearly the considerable success of the efforts and wiles of Satan; yet, "the firm foundation of God stands." The Holy Spirit states in Zechariah 4:10, "For who hath despised the day of small things".

Thus, while we can take into account Christian growth, faithfulness to God is wonderfully pleasing to Heaven[26]—the word

---

[26] "His lord said to him, Well, good and faithful bondman, thou wast faithful over a few things, I will set thee over many things: enter thou into the joy of thy lord" (Matthew 25:23)

to those of Philadelphia in Revelation 3 is "thou hast a little power, *and hast kept my word,* and hast not denied my name." Conversely, the word to those of Laodicea is "thou art lukewarm, and neither cold nor hot, I am about to spue thee out of my mouth." I shudder at that and yet there are evidently those in Christendom today like that—lukewarm.

A Heavenly People

Ultimately, then, these matters of our new nature as born again, the indwelling and capacitating power of the Holy Spirit, our fidelity to Christ and our fidelity to the truth (which is the same thing as He Himself is "the truth") and to other Christians in love and affection—and, lateral truths which we have been discussing—form the very foundation of Scriptural teaching as to our testimonial path here as a heavenly people. Also, in respect of our eternal home, these truths help fit us— through intelligent understanding[27]—for that very day when we enter into our eternal, heavenly home together. There will be no breakdown in Heaven, no variation in understanding, no denominations, no error, no conflict—in short, nothing of our failures as Christians on earth. God's clear desire, as we have been laboring to highlight in this book, is that we understand our heavenly calling *now* and, in the light of that understanding, properly enter into our Christian testimony while yet here on earth. James writes in the first chapter of his epistle, "Pure and undefiled religion before God and the Father is this: …. to keep oneself unspotted from the world." Do any yet not understand that Christianity is a heavenly calling? We cannot stay unspotted from the world if we are immersed in worldly pursuits and pleasures. Are any yet vague as to the reality that proper unity under the hand of the Holy Spirit is God's desire for us even while yet on this earth? Is there a lack of clarity as to the incredible reality of a nature being introduced, through new birth, that is without sin? Do any think that God expects us to meander along in sin? Or, is the Bible

---

[27] "the knowledge of the Holy is intelligence" (Proverbs 9:10)

clear that we are to be overcomers here and, as such, any sin, speaking intelligently, could be likened more to a constitutionally healthy man being subject at intervals to the influences of a cold or the flu in distinction to a willful sinner whom we could liken, in this analogy, to a man who is suffused with cancer?

What does it say at the close of Ecclesiastes in chapter 12? "Let us hear the end of the whole matter: Fear God, and keep his commandments; for this is the whole of man." God is seeking that we understand the end—and, from this we can be helped to work out the beginning and the middle. Ecclesiastes 7:8 shows this clearly—"Better is the end of a thing than its beginning." Why do Christians take so long to arrive at God's thoughts for us? The answer can only be this—"self" intervenes. It is noteworthy that the children of Israel spent almost 40 years in the wilderness (this is our present occupation—moving through the moral wilderness of this scene here); yet, it says at the very beginning of Deuteronomy (a book that in many ways encapsulates Israel's history in the wilderness), "There are eleven days' journey from Horeb by the way of mount Seir to Kadesh-barnea" (Deuteronomy 1:2). Eleven days!! Yet, through murmurings and failures it took some 40 years. Stephen said to his fellow Jews in Acts 7, "O stiffnecked and uncircumcised in heart and ears, ye do always resist the Holy Spirit; as your fathers, ye also."

We need to see clearly as to our Christian calling and circumstances. The Lord said to the Pharisees in Matthew 16, "When evening is come, ye say, Fine weather, for the sky is red; and in the morning, A storm to-day, for the sky is red [and] lowering; ye know [how] to discern the face of the sky, but ye cannot the signs of the times." The query to Jeremiah the prophet was, "What seest thou, Jeremiah?" (Jeremiah 1:11). The blind man initially saw men as trees walking (Mark 8:24)—with the Lord's second touch he then "saw distinctly, and was restored and saw all things clearly." We should see and understand clearly—this is our Christian portion. The Lord said to His own when here, "To you it is given *to know* the mysteries of the kingdom of God"—this is our portion and may it be so. Paul succinctly writes, "We have the mind of Christ" (1 Corinthians 2:6)—an immense reality—and we are told to be "leading captive every thought into the obedience of the Christ" (2 Corinthians 10:5). These are powerful realities!

We must, of course, acknowledge, as already mentioned, that there is a growth factor with Christians (see 1 John 2 as to "children", "young men" and "fathers"—recognizing, however, that we can still see that, whatever the age/growth, understanding and overcoming is expected); however, the end God has in view for each is seen in Ephesians 4:13, "until we all arrive at the unity of the faith and of the knowledge of the Son of God, *at [the] full-grown man*, at [the] measure of the stature of the fulness of the Christ." We must understand the blueprint, speaking reverently, that God fully provides in the Bible and makes real and living to us through the power of the Holy Spirit. We see in Ezekiel 47 that the prophet entered into the river initially to his ankles; but, that, ultimately, it was "waters to swim in." Are we "ankle-deep" Christians; or, preferably, have we come into the full depths of Christianity?

The great moral view in Scripture is manhood—which is to say, *not* children. This is a challenge to us all. Are we standing in manhood before God? Paul wrote to the Corinthians that he had "not been able to speak to you as to spiritual, but as to fleshly; as to babes in Christ. I have given you milk to drink, not meat, for ye have not yet been able, nor indeed are ye yet able"—what a telling word! Christian manhood (a moral stature not necessarily linked, speaking intelligently, to literal age) involves committal to Christ. Paul writes in 2 Timothy 2:4 that "No one going as a soldier entangles himself with the affairs of life, that he may please him who has enlisted him as a soldier." Associated with this, as touched upon earlier, is the simple reality that we need to become, at least in acceptable degree, students of scripture—"give thyself to reading" (1 Timothy 4:13). How can a Christian display and stand for Christ in this "present evil world" if he or she does not properly know at least foundational doctrine of scripture on the subject of Christian character and calling?

Lastly, as we have been reiterating, we have to stand for the truth, come what may—"For this reason take [to you] the panoply of God, that ye may be able to withstand in the evil day, and, *having accomplished all things, to stand*" (Ephesians 6:13). We can see from the mighty men of David (2 Samuel 23) that they were set to be overcomers. It says, for example, of Eleazar the son of Dodo the son of an Ahohite that "He arose and smote the Philistines until his hand was weary, and his hand clave to the sword" (2 Samuel 23:10). This is challenging to us—do we know anything of contending for the truth according to the mind of the Lord to the result that we won't be overcome? His hand "clave" to the sword. Of course, we are not seeking to slay others; but, the moral principle involved is clear enough and we have "the sword of the Spirit, which is God's word" (part of the panoply of Ephesians 6). We've already quoted Jude's words, "Beloved, using all diligence to write to you of our common salvation, I have been obliged to write to you *exhorting [you] to contend earnestly for the faith* once delivered to the saints."

I firmly believe, as I have been constantly emphasizing, that the single biggest hindrance to any of us in our Christian path is lack of fidelity. We are a heavenly people and form the Bride of Christ. Fidelity draws us closer to the Lord, and, even in natural relationships, such intimacy through nearness results in a deepened understanding. Mary of Magdala's heart in respect of the Lord was such that she would not leave the tomb until she had found the body of the Lord. As a result, she received directly from the Lord one of the greatest messages in the history of mankind—"go to my brethren and say to them, I ascend to my Father and your Father, and [to] my God and your God" (John 20:17). We have another lovely example as to this in John 13—"Now there was at table one of his disciples in the bosom of Jesus, whom Jesus loved. Simon Peter makes a sign therefore to him to ask who it might be of whom[28] he spoke. But he, *leaning on the breast of Jesus*, says to him, Lord, who is it?" The Lord then gave the answer.

When the Holy Spirit makes plain any feature of the truth and we divert from that—are we not displaying that same spirit of independency that caused Adam and Eve to fail in the Garden of Eden those many centuries ago? We should, rather, be like the servant in Exodus 21 who "shall say distinctly, I love my master, my wife, and my children, I will not go free; then his master shall bring him before the judges, and shall bring him to the door, or to the door-post; and his master shall bore his ear through with an awl; and he shall be his bondman for ever." The principle is clear enough. Are we prepared to serve the Lord in this way? He has, and continues to, serve us in this way—"No one has greater love than this, that one should lay down his life for his friends." Consider, as well, the blessed service of the Holy Spirit—God Himself—who, in infinite downstooping, has taken a place within the heart and person

---

[28] i.e., His betrayer—who, of course, was Judas Iscariote

of the redeemed Christian for all eternity! We should be decided in our minds to be overcomers—those who "Strive diligently to present thyself approved to God, a workman that has not to be ashamed, cutting *in a straight line* the word of truth" (2 Timothy 2:15).

There is great liberation from harmful influences here when we are faithful to our heavenly calling—faithful to the Lord—faithful like Mary of Magdala to the love that sought and claimed us. Faithfulness in our relationship with Divine Persons produces intelligence, liberty and authority[29]—and thus we can also be generally preserved from the griefs and repercussions of earthly failures. Again, I emphasize that none of us—even the brightest Christians—are going to walk through this scene and never sin. But, that in no way mitigates the fact that God has set us up with the power and the resources to walk here as overcomers—the great challenge is whether we have the affection towards Christ to be faithful in every way. It is akin to the tennis coach, if you will, coaching the athlete to produce winning shots every time. There are no illusions as to the reality that some points in the match will not be won. But, the thrust of the teaching is to seek to achieve the result that the tennis player *will* win every point.

We have already mentioned that, if we are faithful to God, we will certainly be faithful, as a reflex, to the brethren. The first epistle of John sets out this very subject—love and faithfulness. It has been well said that John's writings form the backbone of Scripture. John writes, "And this commandment have

---

[29] "And Jehovah said, Shall I hide from Abraham what I am doing? ....
For I know him that he will command his children and his household after him, and they shall keep the way of Jehovah, to do righteousness and justice" (Genesis 17:18,19)

we from him, That he that loves God love also his brother" (1 John 4:21).

Is it not troublesome and concerning that Christians meet each other as they move through the corridors of life, so to speak—and, yet, are then separate in fellowship from each other in their individual Christian circumstances? There is a myriad of denominations and splinter fellowships. Some estimate over 30,000 which cannot be accurate; but, nevertheless, this gives the sense of the tremendous disparity. I can say that, for myself, it is a pressing and abiding concern—a grief, really—that Christians are so divided. Paul writes in 1 Corinthians 1:10, " Now I exhort you, brethren, by the name of our Lord Jesus Christ, that ye all say the same thing, and that there be not among you divisions; but that ye be perfectly united in the same mind and in the same opinion."

What to Do?

As we referenced earlier in this book—do we have any recourse in respect to all the public breakdown in Christendom? Would God leave us without resources and mandates as to broken times? The answer to the first question is "yes" and to the second question "no", and we have already quoted earlier "The firm foundation of God stands" (2 Timothy 2:19). This section of scripture in second Timothy has been appropriately referred to as the Christian charter for broken times. Paul wrote it when "all who are of Asia .... have turned away from me"—the great public breakdown of the Church had commenced. Think of the labors of this great servant—only to see this declension. Yet, it had been foretold by both the Lord and by Paul himself—"grievous wolves" would come in, not sparing the flock.

Paul instructs us in this chapter in 2 Timothy 2 as to the divinely given path when unjudged error, confusion and declension take place: "Yet the firm foundation of God stands, having this seal, [The] Lord knows those that are his; and, Let every one who names the name of [the] Lord withdraw from iniquity. But in a great house there are not only gold and silver vessels, but also wooden and earthen; and some to honour, and some to dishonour. If therefore one shall have purified himself from these, [in separating himself from them], he shall be a vessel to honour, sanctified, serviceable to the Master, prepared for every good work. But youthful lusts flee, and pursue righteousness, faith, love, peace, with those that call upon the Lord out of a pure heart."

We can note several elements here. First, Christendom today
is a "great house" and we cannot *leave* the house. But, within
the house are various types of persons: true Christians—some
walking righteously and some less so or not at all—and then
we must also include, for practical purposes, professing Christians. Some of the vessels in the house are to honor, and some
to dishonor. If what is dishonorable to God cannot and will
not be judged by Christians in any given fellowship—then, the
apostle Paul mandates to Timothy and to us that we must separate from what is wrong. The Greek word rendered "puri-
fied/separate" means "to cleanse thoroughly; to purge out"
and the Bible translator's note here is of help since some have
had confusion as to this phrase: "The word for purified is only
found here and 1 Corinthians 5:7, `Purge out.' There it was to
get rid of the old leaven out of the lump; here the one who
names the name of the Lord has to purge himself from among
the vessels. Hence we have an additional preposition which is
rendered by `separating from.'  Literally, `purified himself
away from these'."

The next thing to notice is that the Christian who righteously,
according to such appropriate scripture, separates himself or
herself is on individual lines here—it is not a question of what
the next fellow does or doesn't do. It is a question of what is
morally right before the Lord for each of us. The righteous
Christian is to separate from others who, themselves, refuse
to make necessary, right judgments as to some unscriptural
activity, etc. The separated Christian is then (and, by extrap-
olation, only then) "sanctified and serviceable to the Master."
This is a very simple aspect of the truth—we cannot pretend
to be of proper service to the Lord if we are linked with what
does not agree with Scripture. The apostle Paul wrote, "Do ye
not know that a little leaven leavens the whole lump? Purge

out the old leaven, that ye may be a new lump, according as ye are unleavened" (1 Corinthians 5:6.7). Leaven in Scripture always refers to the unwanted influence of the old man—in the OT types we can see that it was always to be excluded from any of the offerings[30] (see Leviticus 2:11). We cannot as Christians be associated with what is wrong and not suffer an influence from that—"Evil communications corrupt good manners" (1 Corinthians 15:33).

The third step in Paul's teaching here in 2 Timothy 2 is that the separate Christian is to find others who have also separated from what might hinder—and to "pursue righteousness, faith, love, peace, with those that call upon the Lord out of a pure heart." We have to note that righteousness is listed first—for a reason. This is shown in Scripture to be the proper ground of fellowship in the OT and at any time in our Christian epoch—i.e., separate from what is wrong and be in proper association with what is right.

We must, again, pay special attention that these moral injunctions are directed to one "who names the name of [the] Lord." This doesn't just mean that if a Christian has the Lord's name on their lips it will suffice. The Lord has "a name, that which is above every name, that at the name of Jesus every knee should bow, of heavenly and earthly and infernal [beings]" (Philippians 2:9,10). Immense respect and obedience are due to that Name! It is what is integral to that Name—holiness, moral beauty, integrity. The voice from Heaven proclaimed the Lord—"This is my beloved Son, in whom I have found my

---

[30] There were two circumstances in which leaven was to be included in the offering which represents, as it were, God giving the nod, reverently speaking, to the reality that, as men here on earth, the leaven exists.

delight" (Matthew 3:17). Let not any think that Heaven has any casual regard for that Name—and, neither are we to be casual in any respect.

As a final note in reference to this principle of maintaining righteousness in God's house—which the Bible presents throughout from the OT through the NT—it is of interest that, in the type (the tabernacle system in the OT) doorkeeping was emphasized. We see in 2 Chronicles 23:19 that "And he set the doorkeepers at the gates of the house of Jehovah, that no one *unclean in anything should enter in.*" This moral principle is as in force today as it was all those centuries ago. Who are the doorkeepers today? You and I!

The Scripture is filled with mandates and precepts as to right and wrong; but, it is helpful in matters of righteousness to understand the *principle* involved in recognizing sin. We have already quoted much earlier in this book as to the definition of sin—"sin is lawlessness". This, as we have seen, means that any activity of the "old man" which will be in contradiction to what is morally due to God is sin. It involves the natural will. We can be considerably helped, therefore, in understanding the moral circumstances due to God by taking a moment to look at the type of the leper in Leviticus 13. Leprosy in the Bible always indicates what is morally unclean and represents, essentially, the rampant activity of the flesh. For us as Christians, of course, the antitype is that the untrammeled activity of "the mind of the flesh" (Romans 8:6) morally is that which intrudes into and causes error and dissension in God's House.

Much detail in Leviticus 13 is given as to how to determine leprosy and then, reflexively, how to adjudicate in relation to the leper. Without going into all the detail, two points should

98

be of interest to us: (1) if there was even "a *trace* of raw flesh" (i.e., the "raw" flesh immediately showing us, in the antitype, that the unregenerate mind of the flesh was active) we are given to understand the sobering reality that, in respect of this activity, only a "trace" was needed to determine that the person was leprous and (2) much care was given, first, to determine if there was indeed leprosy—even to shutting up the leper several times if necessary and then, if it was present, to deal with it. This all highlights the simple reality that God wants His people to be extremely careful in regard to sin[31].

It is necessary to say, of course, that we need to have confidence in the brethren that what is righteous and due to God is being maintained by each and every one. We don't go around peering under shirt sleeves, so to speak, looking for traces of leprosy. However, what is important is that—each of us having been made a priest (Revelation 1:6)—we are (or, should be) fit for the ability to righteously, according to scripture, adjudicate in our own locale regarding any issues of righteousness. As already stated earlier, we start with ourselves; but, we cannot then leave out all the circumstances of our fellowship. In this way, we can maintain what is rightly due to God. As a brother well said many years ago—He wouldn't leave a

---

[31] We are to be careful as to any sin since we are in relationship to a Holy God ("Be careful in his presence, and hearken unto his voice"—Exodus 23:21). However, in respect of the teaching of Leviticus 13 as to leprosy the Bible is setting out in the type a certain, manifest "state" of a soul— i.e., there is present some unhindered, sinful activity of the mind of the flesh. This would differ, using an elemental and understandable example, from a constitutionally righteous Christian man momentarily struck by lust in his heart for a woman—but, then, immediately judging the moment and confessing it to the Lord—in distinction to a Christian engaging in, say, ongoing adultery.

Christian fellowship for any amount of evil (i.e., he wasn't putting a measurement on the immediate *amount* of some evil that might appear); but, he would leave for any amount of *unjudged* evil (i.e., if Christians with whom he was walking refused to judge evil he would leave since, at that point, scriptural precepts and any admonitions from the Holy Spirit were being refused). First Corinthians 5 highlights all of this—incredible evil was being tolerated by that local assembly in allowing the ongoing presence of the incestuous man; but, it is evident from Paul's second epistle that the brethren had adjudicated the matter (they were evidently even overzealous to the result that Paul actually had to remonstrate with them as to receiving back the repentant man).

I trust that what is set out in this brief book is acceptable to those who read it. You will have noticed that I have sought, throughout, that everything stated be grounded in and reinforced by God's Word which "[is] divinely inspired, and profitable for teaching, for conviction, for correction, for instruction in righteousness" (2 Timothy 3:16). Every Christian should properly represent what is of Christ while they are here, and all true Christians should be together in right conditions of fellowship. This is the tenor of the Bible. The power for it is present—God has provided it to each of us at the outset of our Christian path. "Greater is he that [is] in you than he that [is] in the world" (1 John 4:4). In this book I have sought to present these realities so that we can all be helped to understand that, inherently, Christianity is a system according to God "of power, and of love, and of wise discretion" (2 Timothy 1:7). It is important for all to remember that, while we are and will for eternity be of the race of man, we are, also, Sons of the living God. The Lord refers to Himself—although, of course, having many other titles—as Son of Man and Son of God.

All of the above should involve, as already stated, a commensurate joy in doing what is right and pleasing to God. Christianity should not be regarded as burdensome—it is a clear reality, as shown in scripture, that God's blessings are associated with doing what is right. When the children of Israel were entering into Canaan (the promised land) God indicated that there were before them two mountains (the matter was being emphasized—we cannot miss the existence of the mountain): "life and good" which was Mount Gerizim and "death and evil" which was Mount Ebal. What is inculcated by the Holy Spirit always leads us into the fullness of life; what is engendered by the mind of the flesh is leading us into death. "There is a way that seemeth right unto a man, but the end thereof is the ways of death" (Proverbs 14:12).

Christianity should involve for each Christian, as stated, the enjoyment of the relationship. This includes the enjoyment of nearness with Divine Persons, and the taste even now of our eternal inheritance—"Lay hold of eternal life, to which thou hast been called" (1 Timothy 6:12). Any departure in any degree from the relationship results, in corresponding degree, a diminution of our Christian joys, Christian liberty, Christian authority ("the righteous are bold as a lion"—Proverbs 28:1) and Christian testimony.

Thus, we should, as David wrote in Psalm 19, take infinite pleasure in being able to walk properly in the company of the Lord as we move through on our earthly path:

> "The law of Jehovah is perfect, restoring
> the soul; the testimony of Jehovah is sure,
> making wise the simple; The precepts of

101

Jehovah are right, rejoicing the heart; the commandment of Jehovah is pure, enlightening the eyes; The fear of Jehovah is clean, enduring for ever; the judgments of Jehovah are truth, they are righteous altogether: They are more precious than gold, yea, than much fine gold; and sweeter than honey and the dropping of the honeycomb. Moreover, by them is thy servant enlightened; in keeping them there is great reward." Amen.

If you have enjoyed this book, you can find similar writings on this website: www.bible-ministry.com There is contact information there, as well as a large number of some of the finest hymns in Christendom. I would be very interested to hear what any legitimately has to say as to what has been presented. We should all be together here in this world in every locale in love and full fidelity to Christ—not only is it possible, it is scriptural.

A Final Chapter—the World

This final chapter is added as somewhat of an addendum; however, it involves Biblical truths—already incorporated in degree into the main body of this book—as important to our Christian liberty and testimony as any other truths in Scripture. Because of this importance this separate chapter on the world is devoted specifically to it.

There is, perhaps, nothing more pernicious to—nothing that affects more—the distinctiveness of our path in testimony here than for Christians to misunderstand or to ignore the clear, pervasive language of the Bible from beginning to end as to a necessary, moral separation from a world system that is the result of mankind's inherent refusal of God's authority and holiness. This world system has created in the spirit of the unregenerate creature a range of pursuits and pleasures, goals and endeavors, and thoughts and philosophies that have, at their heart, the pride and presumptions of a race of men as to which the Bible says, "every imagination of the thoughts of his heart only evil continually" (Genesis 6:5). Sober language indeed.

James 4:4-5 distinctly states, "know ye not that friendship with the world is enmity with God? Whoever therefore is minded to be [the] friend of the world is constituted enemy of God. Think ye that the scripture speaks in vain? Does the Spirit which has taken his abode in us desire enviously?"

This language is immensely compelling. Don't be in friendship with the world! What does this mean? Is it ok to be immersed in some world-system pursuit created—apart from God—by man according to his own, unregenerate desires? Or, rather, would this, according to this scripture, put you at *enmity* with God? Even being *minded* to be the friend of the world is—what? Constituted *enemy* of God! How could this possibly be interpreted in any way other than what is expressed? Does the language say to be embroiled in the world just as are the unredeemed? Or, does it say *don't*! "*Think ye that the scripture speaks in vain?*" Is the Holy Spirit "which has taken his abode in us" trifling/desiring enviously as to these issues?

There is a conviction with many Christians that God desires that, for whatever time they are left on this earth, they should attempt to rejuvenate a world-system here that has been damaged and changed by the fall of man in the Garden of Eden. However, the Lord said in John 8:23 "*I* am not of this world" and said to His own in John 15:19 "*Ye* are not of the world", and it is clear that the world is only awaiting a future time in which it is going to be burned up (see 2 Peter 3). There will be no peace on this earth until the blessed Peacemaker Himself moves in a final way as shown in the very final chapters of the Bible—Revelation 21 and 22. While the Christian certainly is to promote peace as much as possible in their circumstances ("blessed the peace-makers"—Matthew 5:9) this is simply a result of our Christian estate. To think that any can ultimately make this broken world a substantially better place through any activism or political endeavor is fruitless. The Bible is distinctive in its language—the world is fallen, it is corrupt ("the *present* evil world"—Galatians 1:4)—and God is bearing with it only in view of saving men ("[The] Lord does not delay his promise, as some account of delay, but is longsuffering towards you, not willing that any should perish, but that all should come to repentance"—2 Peter 3:9). There are many that might take exception to these statements; however, Titus 2:12-13 shows us that "that, having denied impiety and worldly lusts, we should live soberly, and justly, and piously in the present course of things, awaiting the blessed hope and appearing of the glory of our great God and Saviour Jesus Christ." Our hope and our place is elsewhere—not, in this world.

We have to bear in mind, always, God's intent in his primary thoughts. These thoughts are applicable *in principle* at all times in all circumstances to all men. Occasionally we might be shown some *provisional* allowance as to principles at a *given* time as simply due to God's grace in dealing with a fallen creation; however, this does not mean that God is condoning sin. We see in Acts 17 that Paul preaches "Athenians, in every way I see you given up to demon worship" - something patently wrong - but, then, further on says "God therefore, having overlooked the times of ignorance, now enjoins men that they shall all everywhere repent". Does the *overlooking* of God mean that He was in favor of demon worship; or, does it mean, as we have just quoted that, "The] Lord does not delay his promise, as some account of delay, but is *longsuffering* towards you, not willing that any should perish, but that all should come to repentance"?

Christians are not viewed in scripture as an earthly people at all, and this book has set out a constant drumbeat as to this fact. We are, of course, presently here in an earthly setting – left here to "work out our salvation with fear and trembling" and to "appear as lights in the world" – but we are a heavenly people – a "peculiar people" (Titus 2:14). Paul writes, "if any one [be] in Christ, [there is] a new creation".

Colossians 3:1–3 illustrates this heavenly side by showing "If therefore ye have been raised with the Christ, seek the things [which are] above, where the Christ is, sitting at [the] right hand of God: have your mind on the things [that are] above, not on the things [that are] on the earth; for ye have died, and your life is hid with the Christ in God."

This teaching is further emphasized in Matthew 6 where the Lord Himself says, "Lay not up for yourselves treasures upon the earth .... but lay up for yourselves treasures in heaven .... for where thy treasure is, there will be also thy heart." Our tendency is to seek both heavenly and worldly treasures; but, the worldly side clearly will detract from the heavenly—the Lord clearly explains this in Matthew 6:24 where he says, "No one can serve two masters; for either he will hate the one and will love the other, or he will hold to the one and despise the other. *Ye cannot serve God and mammon.*"

We must balance—lest we think we are to eschew even rightly appointed natural joys here—that it is our "God who affords us all things richly for [our] enjoyment" (1 Timothy 6:17). Thus, there is what God has built into creation and as to which it is our privilege to partake—the enjoyment of good food, the enjoyments of marriage and family, a lovely day at the beach, etc. However, these enjoyments are to be taken up in the light of scriptural and moral teachings—we are not to be gluttons (already mentioned earlier—see Proverbs 23:21), the marriage bed is to be undefiled (Hebrews 13:4), family is not to have pre-eminence over our responsibilities towards God (see, as an example, 1 Kings 1:5-6), we are not to make beach days an idol, etc. Paul writes, as an example of the above principle, "Meats for the belly, and the belly for meats; but God will bring to nothing both it and them" (1 Corinthians 6:13)—i.e., these are all passing realities and are to be taken up with proper appreciation and piety.

This fact as to our heavenly position and change from an earthly stature is quite possibly the least understood reality in Christendom with many if not most Christians. As already quoted, the Lord distinctly says in John 15 "If ye were of the world, the world would love its own; *but because ye are not of the world*, but I have chosen you out of the world". The apostle Paul writes in 1st Corinthians 15, "But that which is spiritual [was] not first, but that which is natural, then that which is spiritual: the first man out of [the] earth, made of dust; the second man, out of heaven. Such as he made of dust, such also those made of dust; and *such as the heavenly [one], such also the heavenly [ones]*." This language shows a present reality. In the Book of Matthew the Lord used the phrase "the kingdom of the heavens" no less than thirty-one times, and said in Matthew 16:19, "And I will give to thee the keys of the kingdom of the heavens; and whatsoever thou mayest bind upon the earth shall be bound in the heavens; and whatsoever thou mayest loose on the earth shall be loosed in the heavens" (see also Matthew 18:18). This is an amazing and powerful statement showing, as it does, that our place in authority as God's sons in the kingdom of the heavens is indeed a present reality. This is not something abstract—it is scripture. The binding, of course, is a *spiritual* binding.

This all brings in another, lateral reality (stated a number of times earlier in this book)—which is that Christianity is, ultimately, a spiritual system. We're in a flesh and blood condition currently; but the apostle Paul concludes the section quoted above in 1st Corinthians 15 by saying, "And as we have borne the image of the [one] made of dust, we shall bear also the image of the heavenly [one]. But this I say, brethren, that *flesh and blood cannot inherit God's kingdom*, nor does corruption inherit incorruptibility." We know that "flesh and blood", as just stated, involves our current bodily form; however, there are considerable moral overtones also present in these statements.

We shall have a change of the body to suit our heavenly home ("We shall not all fall asleep, but we shall all be changed, in an instant, in [the] twinkling of an eye, at the last trumpet") when we leave this earth to be forever with the Lord; but, it is another present reality and constantly emphasized in this book that the Lord said, "God [is] a spirit; and they who worship him must worship him in spirit and in truth" (John 4:24). We do well to state again that Christianity is a system which is present for now on earth—governed here in the power of the Holy Spirit and of which Christ is the Center and Head. The apostle Paul writes in Ephesians, "in whom ye also are built together for a habitation of God in [the] Spirit." This is a present truth – it is not awaiting our entrance into Heaven although that will be the fullest realization of this lovely provision of God.

These spiritual realities are meant by God to elevate us in our mind, our hearts, our spirits and our Christian testimonial path here. This is not anything mystical – it is simply what God presents to us in scripture to enlighten us with our heavenly calling.

According to scripture, then, we are not now morally and by our heavenly calling *of* this world – the Lord "gave himself for our sins, so that he should deliver us *out of* the present evil world, according to the will of our God and Father" (Galatians

108

1:4), and we are longer to be "conformed *to* this world" (Romans 12:2) although still in it physically. We have already set out that there is an infinite moral divide between man in his natural, unregenerate estate – with the accompanying world system man has built that "lies in the wicked one" (1 John 5:19) – and a God who Himself "is light, and in him is no darkness at all" (1 John 1:5). As Christians God has now through new birth and the indwelling power of the Holy Spirit "made us fit for sharing the portion of the saints in light, who has delivered us from the authority of darkness, and translated [us] into the kingdom of the Son of his love" (Colossians 1). We have now been brought, so to speak, onto God's side of the divide.

If we properly grasp the enormity of these elevating truths, they will deliver us from undue entanglement in this world system and its affairs. Many Christians, as already mentioned, endeavor to fix this world; however, God has already judged it in the Cross of Christ ("Now is [the] judgment of this world" – John 12) and it but awaits the practical implementation of this judgment as already indicated in 2nd Peter 3. We are, of course, not hermits—Paul writes as to this in 1 Corinthians 5:10, saying that "since then ye should go out of the world." We are certainly called upon to pull our neighbor's sheep out of the well, to act as good Samaritans, etc.—we are rubbing elbows with our fellow man in our day-to-day affairs year in and year out; but, our Christian testimony should be that "they think it strange that ye run not with [them] to the same sink of corruption" (1st Peter 4) and that we are a people that morally "dwell alone" (Numbers 23:9).

Many Christians are vigorously engaged, as alluded to in prior paragraphs, in the social and entertainment characters of this world system. There is much idolatry in these features of the world, and, as such, all of it is under God's judgment and to be consumed by fire. This latter reality is explicitly set out, as referenced in prior paragraphs, in 1 Peter 3—and it does us well to consider in full what the apostle writes in that section, "But the present heavens and the earth by his word are laid up in store, kept for fire unto a day of judgment and destruction of ungodly men .... But the day of [the] Lord will come as a thief, in which the heavens will pass away with a rushing noise, and [the] elements, burning with heat, shall be dissolved, and [the] earth *and the works in it* shall be burnt up. All these things then being to be dissolved, *what ought ye to be in holy conversation and godliness"*.

There is, then, much occupation with many Christians with politics, the arts, literature, the world of sports, the world of music and entertainment—and, other facets of a world system fashioned by man and morally apart from God. It is all part of a scene of corruption out from which God is, as already shown in this paper, delivering us. Could any legitimately argue that these elements in the world are not rife with idolatry and corruption? There is momentous idolatry[32] connected with sports, music, entertainment and the rest. It is all defined in 1 John 2:15 – 17—" Love not the world, *nor the things in the world.* If any one love the world, the love of the Father is not in him; because *all that [is] in the world*, the *lust of the flesh,* and the *lust of the eyes,* and the *pride of life*, is not of the Father, but is of the world. And the world is passing, and its lust, but he that does the will of God abides for eternity." How

---

[32] Anything, of course, can become an idol. Paul writes to the Corinthians that "we know that an idol [is] nothing in [the] world". It is of considerable interest that in Habakkuk 2:18 it is shown that the word translated "idol" means "nonentity".

could any argue against this? We must see everything from the Divine perspective, and we have this ability through the power of the indwelling Holy Spirit.

It is our nature to say, "Oh, when the Holy Spirit sets out as to *lust* or *the pride of life*—He didn't mean *my focus* on football, or the movies, or music, etc.—He meant something with which the other guy is unduly engaged." When Jeremiah was shown two baskets of figs the Holy Spirit records that one basket had very good figs and one basket very bad figs "which could not be eaten for badness." This was God's estimation of the two baskets. Jeremiah was then asked, "What seest thou, Jeremiah? And I said, Figs: the good figs very good; and the bad very bad, which cannot be eaten for badness." His estimation was identical to that of the Holy Spirit. Here is a clarion statement: *There are no gray areas in regard to the truth—in respect of Christianity*! The principle shown in the figs is that they were either good (in which case they were very good) or, bad (very bad)—*and couldn't be eaten for badness*! How can we turn around after having been delivered from the world and start to feed again on the bad figs? What does the Scripture say? "[The] dog [has] turned back to his own vomit; and, [The] washed sow to [her] rolling in mud" (2 Peter 2:22). Our natural tendency is to soften judgments—we would like to say that the bad figs are not so bad; or, that some of them are good. But, we cannot seek to morally shave or to modify God's estimation as to anything. God's word to us in respect of this says, "Strive diligently to present thyself approved to God, a workman that has not to be ashamed, cutting in a straight line the word of truth" (2 Timothy 2:15). *It is a straight line.* One side is truth—the other side is not the truth. The Lord said, "No one having laid his hand on [the] plough and looking back is fit for the kingdom of God" (Luke 9:62).

Could any plough a straight line while looking back? The Israelites were delivered from the bondage of Egypt; but, they then murmured for Egypt's leeks and onions (see Numbers 11:4-5). This is like ourselves. In the Bible Egypt represents the world system—we appreciate being saved from it and given eternal life; but, our natural tendency is to then want to continue to enjoy the "flavors" of Egypt while we are yet here.

There is nothing evil, speaking generally, in *things*, certainly—"every creature of God [is] good" (1 Timothy 4:4)—but we must constantly balance scripture to ensure that we are properly in possession of the truth. We have already alluded to the fact that the physical appeals and joys in marriage are a wonderful gift from God; but, fornication and adultery are clearly wrong. It is "the God who affords us all things richly for [our] enjoyment" (1 Timothy 6:17); yet, while we can enjoy a good meal, we have mentioned that gluttony is a sin (Proverbs 23:21). We are certainly called upon to make an honest living, to obey the authorities, to be at peace as far as we are able with our fellow man; but, as far as "having part" with such – we are called to be at a moral remove. The language of the Holy Spirit throughout the Bible clearly bespeaks a holy people called out to a holy God and, reflexively and necessarily to be separate morally from a race of men fallen into sin. The second half of 1 Corinthians 6 speaks to this subject in a way that could not be any more direct—and it does us well to consider it here:

"Be not diversely yoked with unbelievers; for what participation [is there] between righteousness and lawlessness? or what fellowship of light with darkness? and what consent of Christ with Beliar, or what part for a believer along with an unbeliever?

and what agreement of God's temple with idols? for ye are [the] living God's temple; according as God has said, I will dwell among them, and walk among [them]; and I will be their God, and they shall be to me a people.

Wherefore come out from the midst of them, and be separated, saith [the] Lord, and touch not [what is] unclean, and I will receive you;

and I will be to you for a Father, and ye shall be to me for sons and daughters, saith [the] Lord Almighty."

This language is overwhelmingly direct. We must notice that the language is to not even "touch" what is morally unclean. These words can be most easily understood by looking at the types in the Old Testament. In the early chapters of Leviticus there is continual language regarding what is "clean" and what is "unclean" so that the Israelite would be separate from and not touch what was unclean. This language for us, in the antitype, involves a practical, *moral* separation—we must remember that Divine *principles* never change and Paul writes in 1 Corinthians 10:11 that "Now all these things happened to them [as] types, and have been written for our admonition, upon whom the ends of the ages are come." We are not bound under the law; but, rather, have been brought into "the perfect law, that of liberty" (James 1:25). However, this is not a liberty to walk in any variation from the mind of God as set out in the unbreakable precepts of scripture.

Daniel is a lovely example of this necessary fidelity to God and divine principles. He was in captivity with his friends in Babylon under the power of Nebuchadnezzar; but, "Daniel purposed in his heart that he would not pollute himself with the king's delicate food, nor with the wine which he drank" (Daniel 1:8). This is a great test to us. The king's delicate food represents the "finer" elements of a natural world system. I recall a few years ago listening to a godly, ministering brother in England speaking to those in his fellowship and admonishing them that rap music was typically ungodly and they shouldn't listen to it (true enough); but, that it was perfectly acceptable to spend an evening listening to Bach at the concert hall. However, it all comes from the same source—a natural world of entertainment—the Bach Symphony, etc. is merely the king's delicate food.

The Lord said when being delivered to the agony of the Cross in John 18, "My kingdom is not of this world; if my kingdom were of this world, my servants had fought that I might not be delivered up to the Jews; but now my kingdom is not from hence." In Luke 9 the disciples suggested to the Lord that they call down fire from heaven to consume a village of the Samaritans who were not receiving the Lord – "turning he rebuked them [and said, *Ye know not of what spirit ye are*]."

What is our spirit/Spirit? It is vital that we understand properly our Christian calling. The Lord said "Ye appear as

114

lights in this world"; but, if our testimony is close to identical with the unbeliever, our lights (notice again that this is "lights"—i.e., the individual side is considered) can become indistinguishable from the confusion of this world. Thus, in The Revelation chapter 3 the Lord says in His address to Laodicea, "because thou art lukewarm, and neither cold nor hot, I am about to spue thee out of my mouth." I trust no honest Christian has any desire to be found as only lukewarm in their testimony here – rather we all should, as already quoted a number of times, "Strive *diligently* to present thyself *approved* to God, a workman that has not to be ashamed, cutting in a straight line the word of truth" (2 Timothy 2).

The difficulty, as is evident, is that we have been left here in a contrary world to work out the practical character of our salvation. As we can see in Revelation 10:10, the words of God are sweet in the mouth; but, in the practical working out of them they are bitter—the old man doesn't like Divine food. We like the salvation and the peace; but, we are challenged as to separating morally from circumstances here to which we are naturally attracted. It is testing to us—and, God intends it to be so.[33] It is to prove our fidelity and our Christian strength of character. The principle as to, reverently speaking, "God first", is seen in Levi's statement as recorded in Deuteronomy 33 all those centuries ago—"Who said to his father and to his mother, I see him not, And he acknowledged not his brethren, And knew not his own children". Yet, Leviticus 19:3 clearly says, "Ye shall reverence every man his mother, and his father." We know that God is not contradicting His own word (see John 10:35)—what is meant by these two scriptures? It

---

[33] "the proving of your faith, much more precious than of gold" (1 Peter 1:7)

is surely easy enough—reverence your father and mother; but, when it comes to any questions as to fidelity to God, He has the first place. The Lord uttered similar words. He was told that His mother and His brethren were without—He said, "for whosoever shall do the will of my Father who is in [the] heavens, he is my brother, and sister, and mother" (Matthew 12:50). As has been repeated throughout this book, everything traces back to the two great commandments—love God fully is the first—the second commandment is, love your neighbor as yourself; *but, these two commandments must be taken up in that order*!

There is a great joy that accrues as a result of being separate from what hinders our relationships with Divine Persons. It involves maintaining the efficacy of the Cross—putting to death in practice the old man that God has removed in the Cross of Christ. The Lord said, "If any one will come after me, let him deny himself and take up his cross daily and follow me" (Luke 9:23). This involves committal to Christ, and it involves manhood—Joshua could say, "as for me and my house, we will serve Jehovah" (Joshua 24:15). May it be so.

Finally, I would like, in closing, to include a hymn written many years ago by a Christian who understood so well this important subject of the world, and the Christian's place morally in relation to the world. If you have never seen it, I trust you enjoy it as much as it has been enjoyed by many before you:

> This world is a wilderness wide;
>
> We have nothing to seek nor to choose;
>
> We've no thought in the waste to abide;

We have nought to regret nor to lose.

For the Lord has Himself gone before;

He has marked out the path that we tread;

It's as sure as the love we adore;

We have nothing to fear nor to dread.

For the path where our Saviour has gone

Has led up to His Father and God,

To the place where He's now on the throne;

And His strength shall be ours on the road.

And with Him shall our rest be on high,

When in holiness bright we sit down,

In the joy of His love ever nigh,

In the peace that His presence shall crown.

'Tis the treasure we've found in His love

That has made us now pilgrims below;

And 'tis there, when we reach Him above,

As we're known, all His fulness we'll know.

And our Saviour! 'tis Thee from on high
We await till the time Thou shalt come,
To take those Thou hast led by Thine eye
To Thyself in Thy heavenly home.

Until then 'tis the path Thou hast trod
Our delight and our comfort shall be;
We're content with Thy staff and Thy rod,
Till with Thee all Thy glory we see.

About the Author

Keith Petersen has been publishing magazine and newspaper articles and stories locally for over 30 years. This is his first foray into publishing a book.

He was raised in a fundamental Christian household, and now lives in a Dutch Colonial directly behind the family house in which his Dad had also been raised and had then bought from *his* mother.

He defiantly left home at 18 and then at the age of 27 surrendered to the pursuing love of the Lord Jesus. Fifteen years later the same grace of God provided him with the blessings of a wife—Caroline. He now has two children—Corinne 21 as this book is published and Daniel 16.

In 1971 he began at the age of 21 working full-time in the local family business started by his Dad in 1956. Today in 2018, he and his brother Doug operate this 62+ year-old business in Central New Jersey, USA.

If this book provides Christian joy and in any further way deepens your sense of all that we as Christians have eternally in Christ; similar ministry as well as some of the loveliest hymns in Christianity can be found at: www.bible-ministry.com